Table of Contents

400+ Facts You Probably Didn't Know About Sports

Hockey, American Football, European Football (Soccer), Basketball, Baseball, and Motorsport Included!

All facts are true at the time of publication. If you notice an error, please contact michellemillerauthor@gmail.com. Thank you for your purchase!

Hockey

1. Ice hockey originated in Canada in the early 19th century.

2. The Stanley Cup is the oldest professional sports trophy in North America

3. Hockey pucks were originally made of wood, with rubber pucks becoming popular in the late 19th century.

4. Hockey pucks are kept frozen until game time.

5. The first organized indoor hockey game was played in Montreal in 1875.

6. The Ottawa Senators were the first team to win the Stanley Cup in the modern era in 1903.

7. Originally, the Stanley Cup was the Canadian amateur hockey championship, only changing to professional teams in 1907.

8. The first professional hockey league, the National Hockey Association (NHA), was established on December 2, 1909.

9. The first-ever NHL game was played on December 19, 1917, between the Montreal Canadiens and Ottawa Senators.

10. The NHL introduced the "loser point" system in the 1921-1922 season, awarding one point for an overtime or shootout loss.

11. The "Original Six" refers to the first six NHL teams: Boston Bruins, Chicago Blackhawks, Detroit Red Wings, Montreal Canadiens, New York Rangers, and Toronto Maple Leafs.

12. The "Original Six" era lasted from 1942 to 1967, after which the league expanded.

13. The "Original Six" teams played a total of 50 regular-season games each year before expansion.

14. The Zamboni was invented by Frank Zamboni in 1949.

15. The "Hat Trick" refers to a player scoring three goals in a single game.

16. The fastest hat trick in NHL history was scored by Bill Mosienko in March 1952 in just 21 seconds.

16. The Detroit Red Wings have a tradition of throwing an octopus onto the ice during games.

17. The first African-American NHL player was Willie O'Ree, who debuted in 1958 with the Boston Bruins.

18. The United States won its first Olympic hockey gold medal in 1960, defeating Canada.

19. Playing for the Boston Bruins Phil Esposito was the first player to score 100 points in a season.

20. The "Broad Street Bullies" were the Philadelphia Flyers teams known for their aggressive playing style in the 1972-1973 season.

21. The "Gordie Howe hat trick" is awarded when a player scores a goal, records an assist, and gets into a fight in a single game.

22. The "Miracle on Ice" from the 1980 Olympic Games is considered a top sports moment. A mainly amateur USA team went on to win the gold medal, despite no one believing they could.

23. The New York Islanders won four consecutive Stanley Cups from 1980 to 1983.

24. The fastest goal in NHL history was scored by Doug Smail, just 5 seconds into a game on December 20, 1981, for the Winnipeg Jets v the St Louis Blues in Winnipeg.

25. The Edmonton Oilers set a record with the most goals in a single NHL season in 1983-1984.

26. The first official women's ice hockey world championship was held in 1990.

27. The NHL introduced video review for goals in the 1991-1992 season.

28. Hockey goaltenders are the only players allowed to have unique designs on their masks, adding a personal touch to their gear.

29. The NHL has had several lockouts, including one that cancelled the entire 2004-2005 season.

30. Anyone can be a goalie! If both NHL goalies are injured in a game, a fan from the stands can step up to take their place.

31. The Montreal Canadiens have won the most Stanley Cups in NHL history, with 24 total wins.

32. Wayne Gretzky, known as "The Great One," holds numerous NHL records, including most career goals and assists.

33. The "Heritage Classic," the NHL's annual outdoor game, was first held in 2003 in Edmonton.

34. The NHL adopted the shootout to decide tied games after overtime starting in the 2005-2006 season.

35. Zdeno Chara has the fastest slapshot recorded in the NHL at 108.8 mph.

36. The NHL's first female referee, Katie Guay, officiated an exhibition game in 2019.

37. The NHL introduced the "coach's challenge" to review certain calls, starting in the 2019-2020 season.

38. Connor McDavid set the record for the fastest skater in NHL All-Star Skills Competition history, with 13.408 seconds in 2024.

39. The "Five Hole" is the space between a goaltender's legs, often targeted by shooters.

40. Hockey sticks are typically made from wood, fibreglass, or a composite material.

41. Hockey rinks are 200 feet long and 85 feet wide, with rounded corners.

42. The ice in hockey rinks is generally ¾ of an inch thick.

43. Another name for the penalty box is the "Sin Bin".

44. The "Flying V" formation, popularized in the movie "The Mighty Ducks," is illegal in the NHL.

45. The "five-minute major" penalty is the longest standard penalty in hockey.

46. Hockey players use a variety of terms, including "dangles" and "snipes," to describe skillful plays and goals.

47. The term "power play" refers to a team having a numerical advantage due to an opponent's penalty.

American
Football

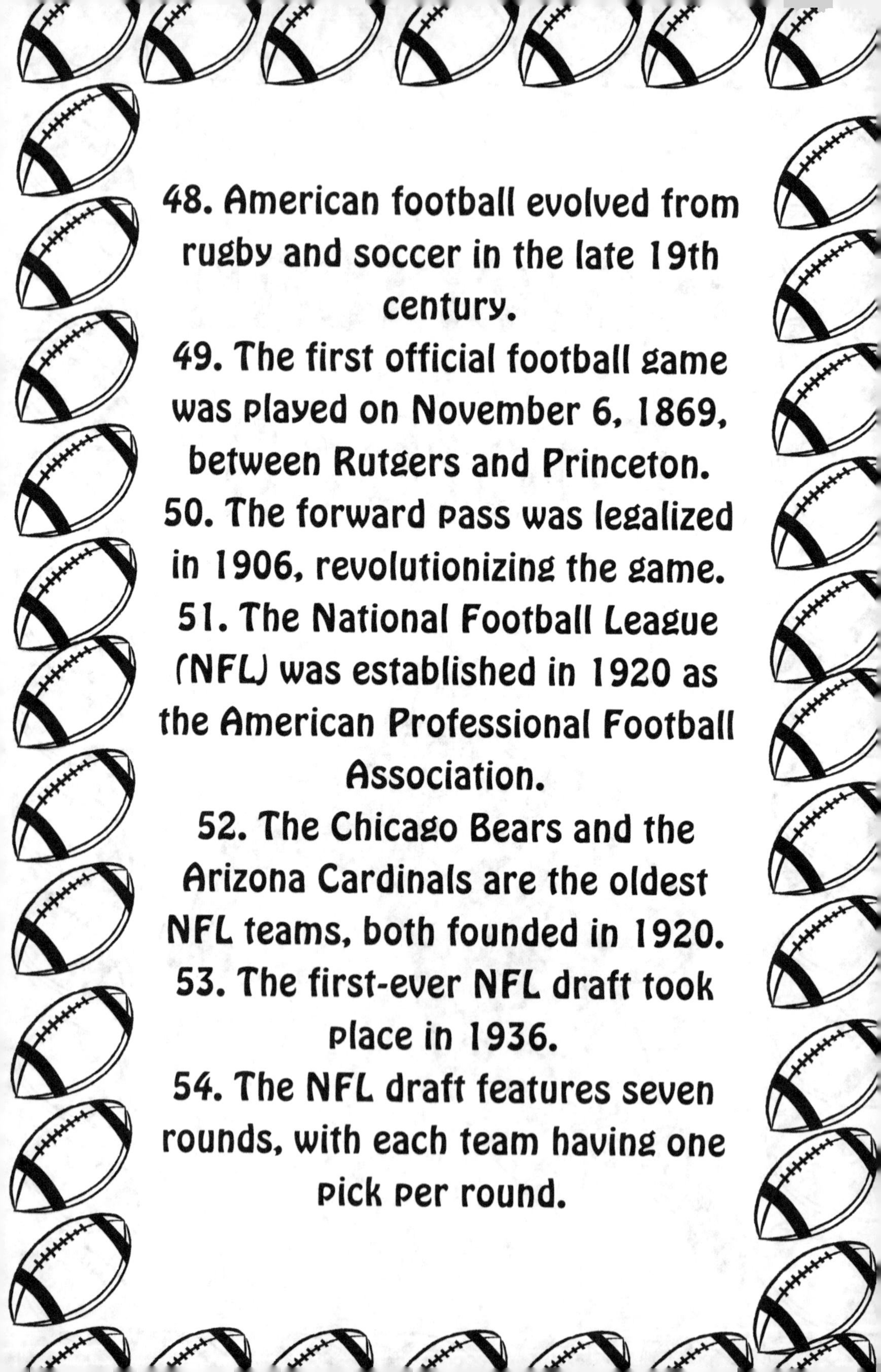

48. American football evolved from rugby and soccer in the late 19th century.

49. The first official football game was played on November 6, 1869, between Rutgers and Princeton.

50. The forward pass was legalized in 1906, revolutionizing the game.

51. The National Football League (NFL) was established in 1920 as the American Professional Football Association.

52. The Chicago Bears and the Arizona Cardinals are the oldest NFL teams, both founded in 1920.

53. The first-ever NFL draft took place in 1936.

54. The NFL draft features seven rounds, with each team having one pick per round.

55. The New Orleans Saints were established in 1967 but did not have a winning season until 1987.

56. The first Super Bowl took place in 1967, and the Green Bay Packers were the champions.

57. The Super Bowl is the most-watched television event in the United States.

58. The Vince Lombardi Trophy is awarded to the winners of the Super Bowl.

59. The Lombardi Sweep, a signature play of the Green Bay Packers, was named after coach Vince Lombardi.

60. The phrase "Super Bowl" was first coined by Lamar Hunt, owner of the Kansas City Chiefs.

61. The Miami Dolphins had a perfect season in 1972, going 17-0.

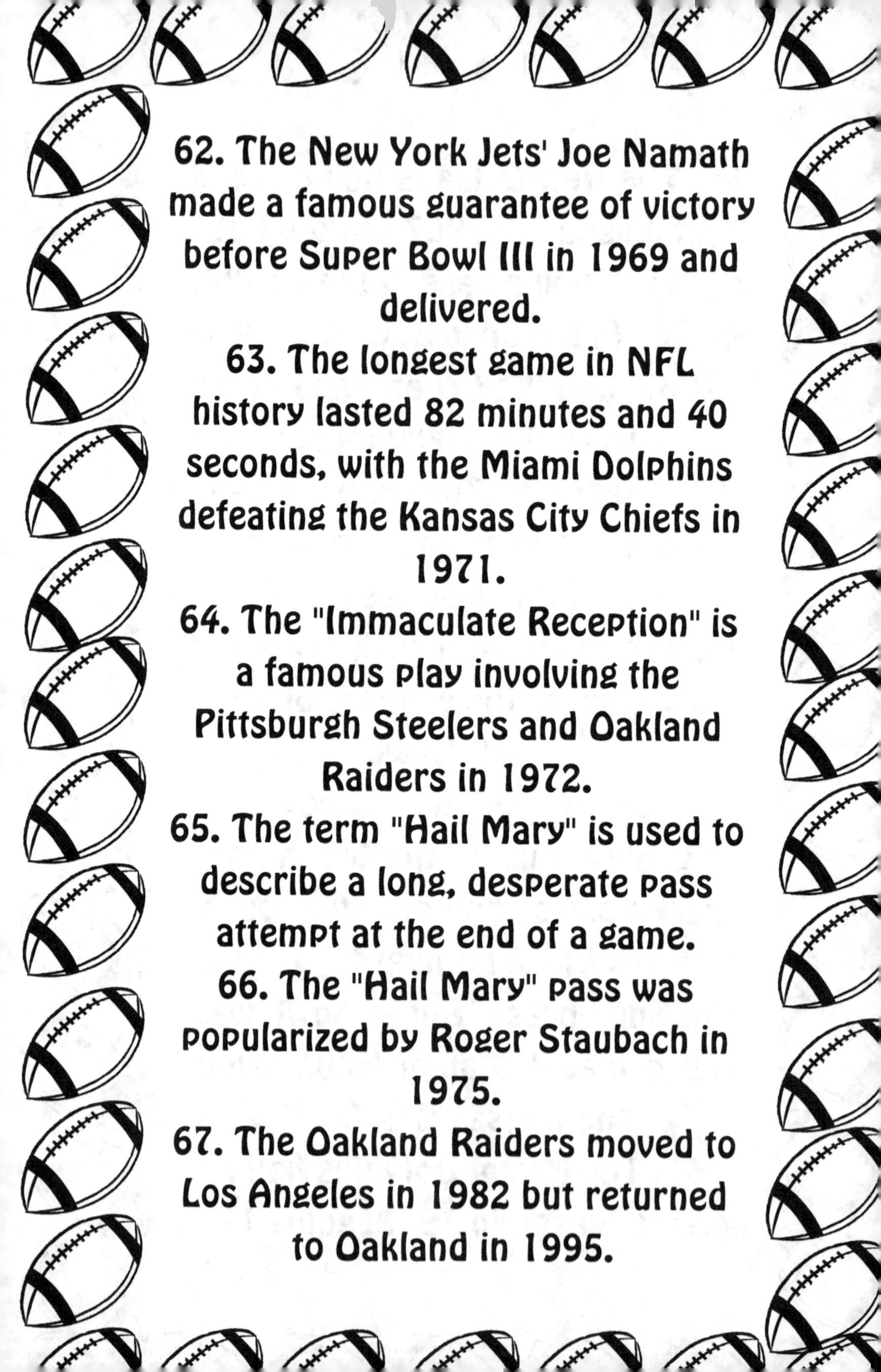

62. The New York Jets' Joe Namath made a famous guarantee of victory before Super Bowl III in 1969 and delivered.

63. The longest game in NFL history lasted 82 minutes and 40 seconds, with the Miami Dolphins defeating the Kansas City Chiefs in 1971.

64. The "Immaculate Reception" is a famous play involving the Pittsburgh Steelers and Oakland Raiders in 1972.

65. The term "Hail Mary" is used to describe a long, desperate pass attempt at the end of a game.

66. The "Hail Mary" pass was popularized by Roger Staubach in 1975.

67. The Oakland Raiders moved to Los Angeles in 1982 but returned to Oakland in 1995.

68. The Indianapolis Colts moved from Baltimore in 1984, causing controversy among fans.

69. The Buffalo Bills appeared in four consecutive Super Bowls from 1990 to 1993 but did not win any.

70. The New England Patriots are known for their "Flying Elvis" logo, introduced in 1993.

71. The "Tuck Rule" controversy occurred during a playoff game between the Oakland Raiders and New England Patriots in 2002.

72. The Houston Texans are the youngest NFL franchise, established in 2002.

73. The NFL Network debuted in 2003, providing 24/7 coverage of the league.

74. The "Butt Fumble" occurred during a game between the New York Jets and the New England Patriots in 2012.

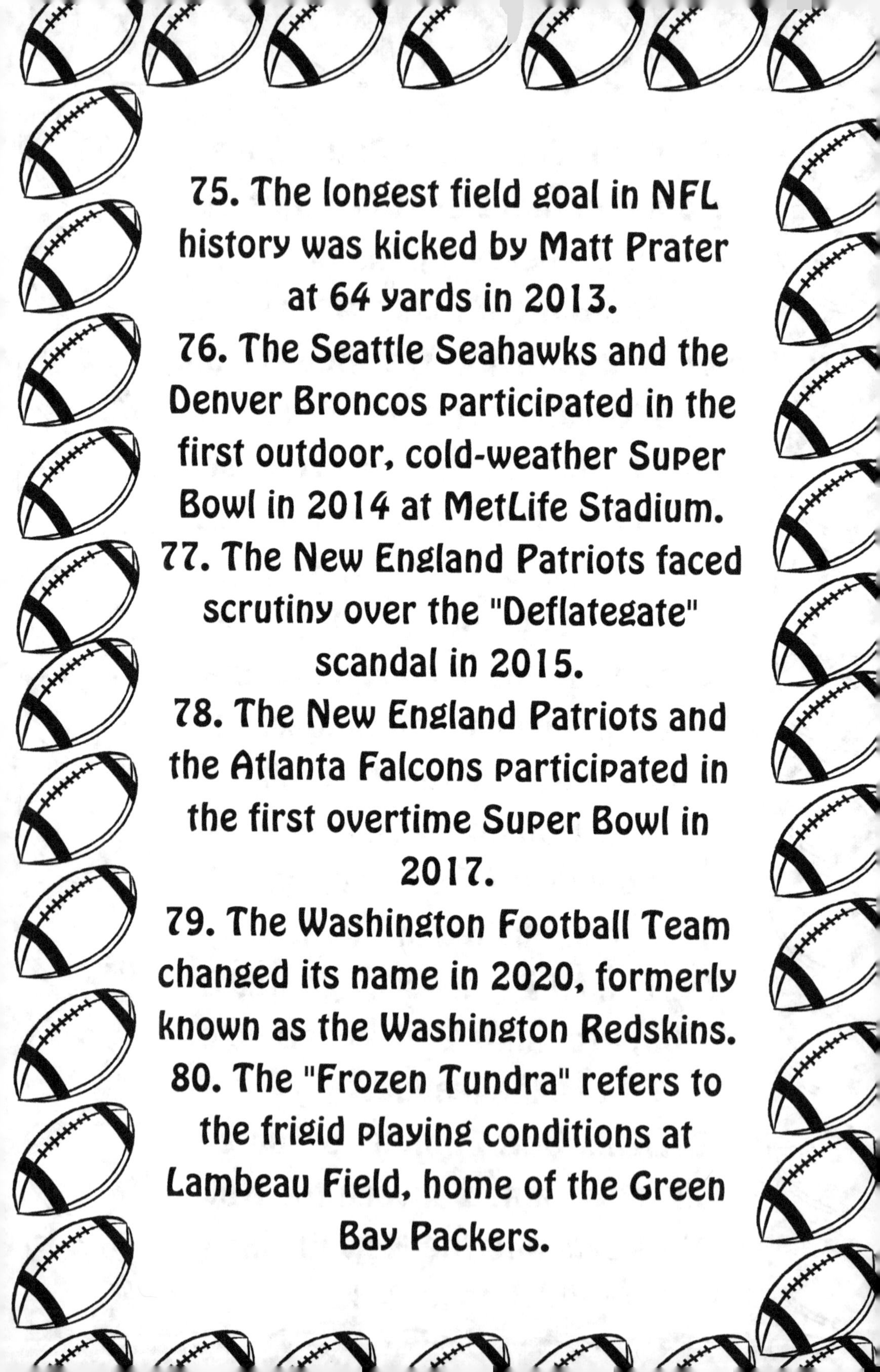

75. The longest field goal in NFL history was kicked by Matt Prater at 64 yards in 2013.

76. The Seattle Seahawks and the Denver Broncos participated in the first outdoor, cold-weather Super Bowl in 2014 at MetLife Stadium.

77. The New England Patriots faced scrutiny over the "Deflategate" scandal in 2015.

78. The New England Patriots and the Atlanta Falcons participated in the first overtime Super Bowl in 2017.

79. The Washington Football Team changed its name in 2020, formerly known as the Washington Redskins.

80. The "Frozen Tundra" refers to the frigid playing conditions at Lambeau Field, home of the Green Bay Packers.

81. The Kansas City Chiefs were named in honour of Kansas City Mayor H. Roe Bartle, nicknamed the "Chief."

82. The Arizona Cardinals are the oldest continuously run professional football team in the United States.

83. The Cincinnati Bengals' mascot is named "Who Dey" after the team's famous cheer.

84. The Atlanta Falcons' mascot is named "Freddie Falcon."

85. The Jacksonville Jaguars' mascot is named "Jaxson de Ville."

86. The Philadelphia Eagles' fight song is titled "Fly, Eagles Fly."

87. The New York Jets' mascot is named "Fireman Ed," a superfan who leads cheers in the stands.

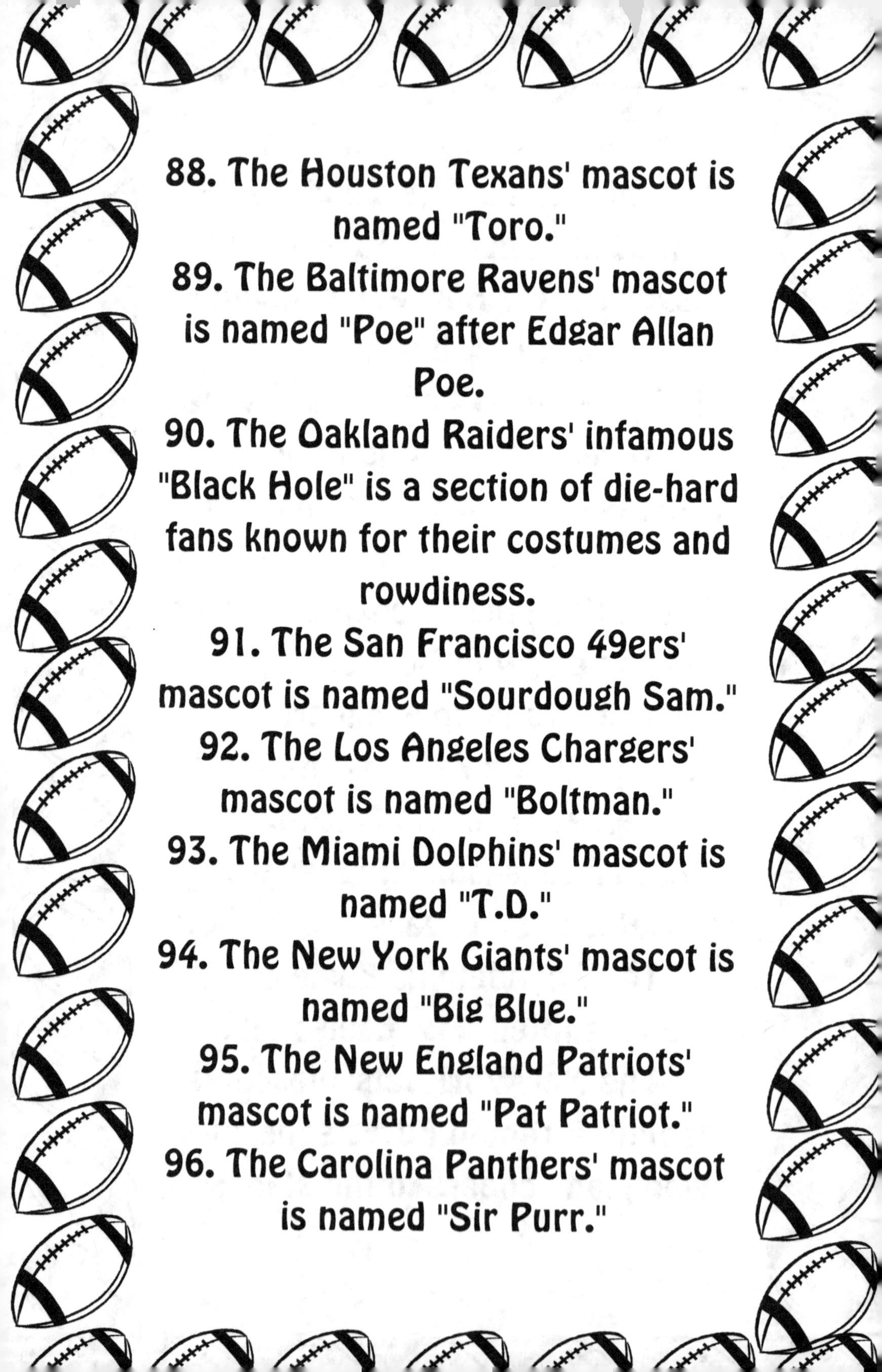

88. The Houston Texans' mascot is named "Toro."

89. The Baltimore Ravens' mascot is named "Poe" after Edgar Allan Poe.

90. The Oakland Raiders' infamous "Black Hole" is a section of die-hard fans known for their costumes and rowdiness.

91. The San Francisco 49ers' mascot is named "Sourdough Sam."

92. The Los Angeles Chargers' mascot is named "Boltman."

93. The Miami Dolphins' mascot is named "T.D."

94. The New York Giants' mascot is named "Big Blue."

95. The New England Patriots' mascot is named "Pat Patriot."

96. The Carolina Panthers' mascot is named "Sir Purr."

97. The Tennessee Titans' mascot is named "T-Rac."

98. The Seattle Seahawks' mascot is named "Blitz."

99. The Chicago Bears' mascot is named "Staley Da Bear."

100. The Dallas Cowboys' mascot is named "Rowdy."

101. The Denver Broncos' mascot is named "Miles."

102. The Indianapolis Colts' mascot is named "Blue."

103. The Kansas City Chiefs' mascot is named "K.C. Wolf."

104. The Minnesota Vikings' mascot is named "Viktor."

105. The Tampa Bay Buccaneers' mascot is named "Captain Fear."

106. The Chicago Bears' fight song is titled "Bear Down, Chicago Bears."

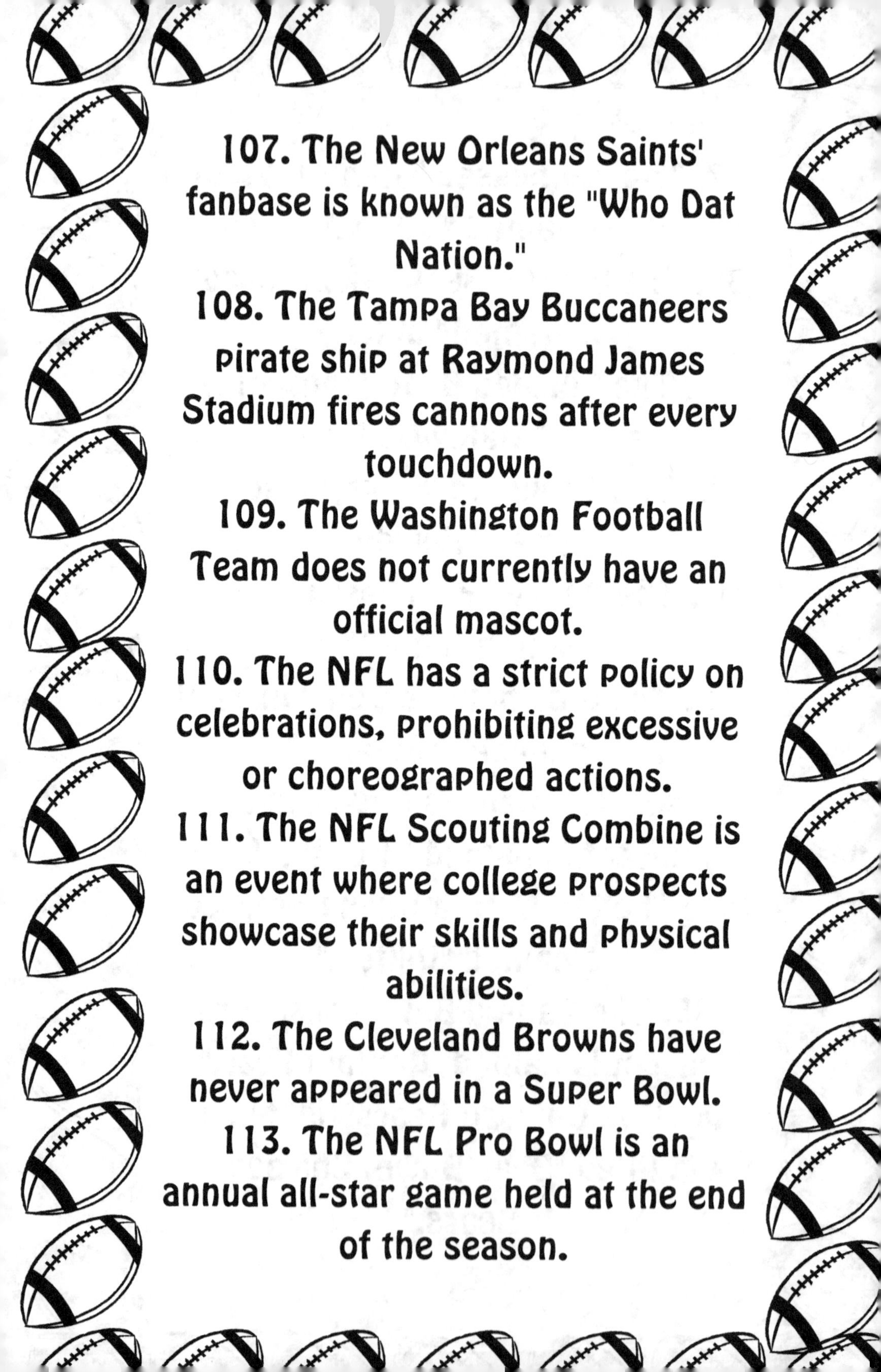

107. The New Orleans Saints' fanbase is known as the "Who Dat Nation."

108. The Tampa Bay Buccaneers pirate ship at Raymond James Stadium fires cannons after every touchdown.

109. The Washington Football Team does not currently have an official mascot.

110. The NFL has a strict policy on celebrations, prohibiting excessive or choreographed actions.

111. The NFL Scouting Combine is an event where college prospects showcase their skills and physical abilities.

112. The Cleveland Browns have never appeared in a Super Bowl.

113. The NFL Pro Bowl is an annual all-star game held at the end of the season.

114. The "No Fun League" is a nickname sometimes used to criticize the NFL's strict rules.

115. The "Hoggettes" are a group of female Washington Football Team fans known for dressing as piglets.

116. The Cleveland Browns' fans are known for wearing paper bags over their heads during tough times.

117. The Cleveland Browns have never appeared in a Super Bowl.

118. The Los Angeles Rams were the first NFL team to have a logo on their helmets.

119. The Green Bay Packers are the only community-owned, non-profit team in the NFL.

120. The NFL has experimented with alternative football leagues, such as the XFL.

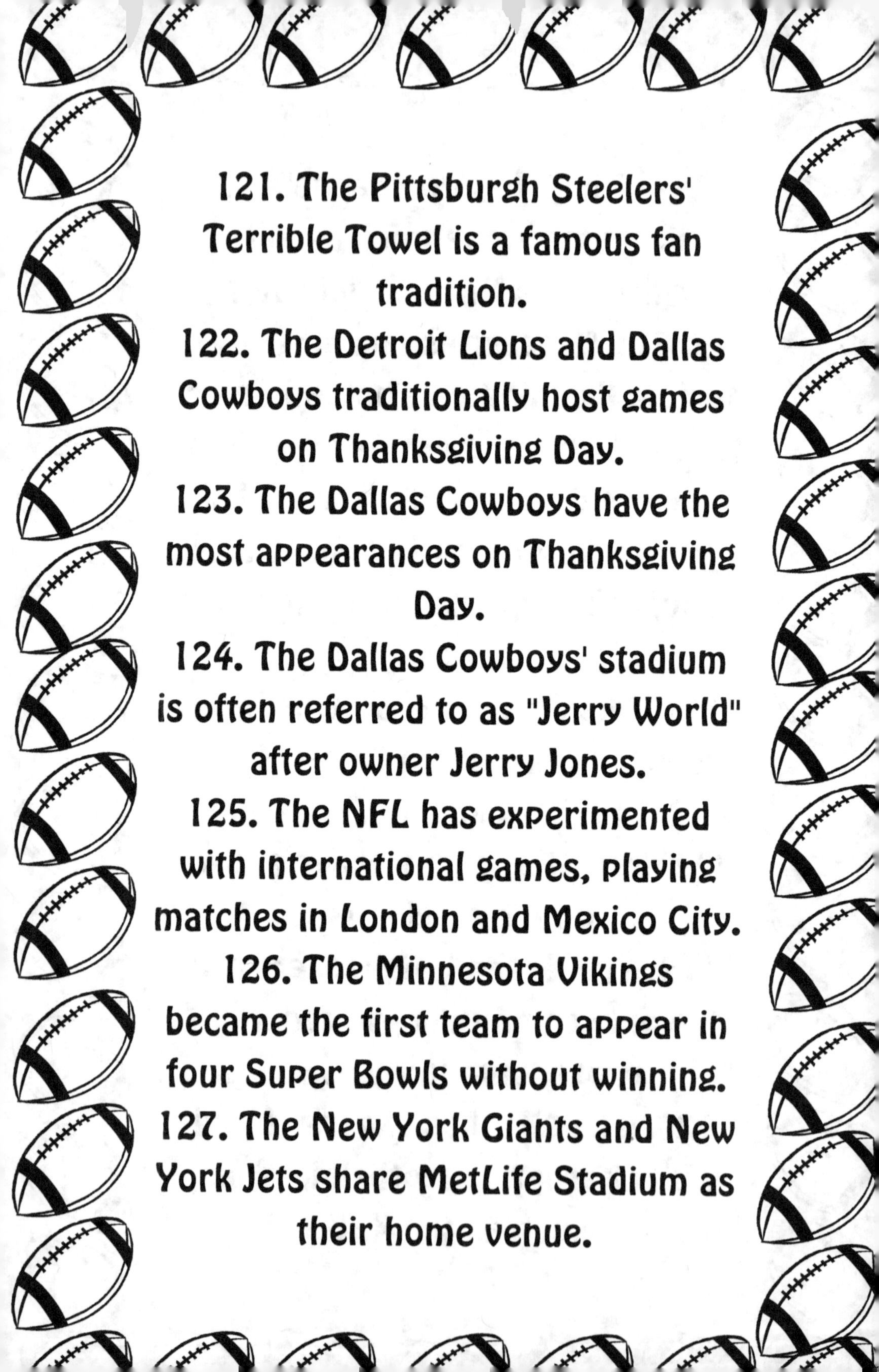

121. The Pittsburgh Steelers' Terrible Towel is a famous fan tradition.

122. The Detroit Lions and Dallas Cowboys traditionally host games on Thanksgiving Day.

123. The Dallas Cowboys have the most appearances on Thanksgiving Day.

124. The Dallas Cowboys' stadium is often referred to as "Jerry World" after owner Jerry Jones.

125. The NFL has experimented with international games, playing matches in London and Mexico City.

126. The Minnesota Vikings became the first team to appear in four Super Bowls without winning.

127. The New York Giants and New York Jets share MetLife Stadium as their home venue.

128. The Baltimore Ravens were named after Edgar Allan Poe's famous poem "The Raven."

129. The official NFL football is made by Wilson Sporting Goods.

130. The longest touchdown pass in NFL history was 99 yards.

131. The New England Patriots and the Pittsburgh Steelers share the record for the most Super Bowl victories by a single team.

132. The Pro Football Hall of Fame is located in Canton, Ohio.

133. The longest field goal in NFL history was kicked by Matt Prater at 64 yards in 2013.

134. The term "gridiron" refers to the hash marks on the field, resembling a grid pattern.

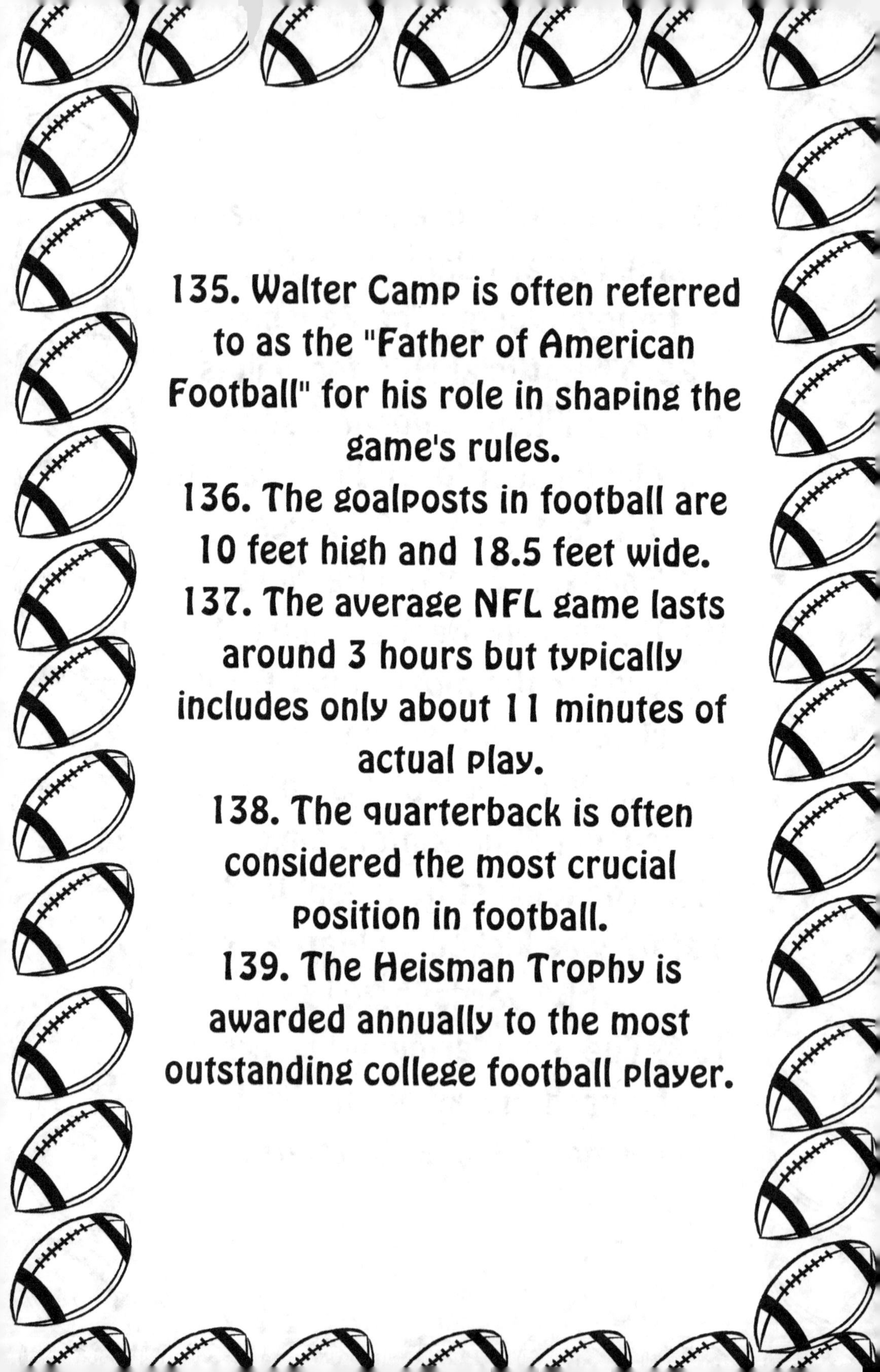

135. Walter Camp is often referred to as the "Father of American Football" for his role in shaping the game's rules.

136. The goalposts in football are 10 feet high and 18.5 feet wide.

137. The average NFL game lasts around 3 hours but typically includes only about 11 minutes of actual play.

138. The quarterback is often considered the most crucial position in football.

139. The Heisman Trophy is awarded annually to the most outstanding college football player.

European
Football
(Soccer)

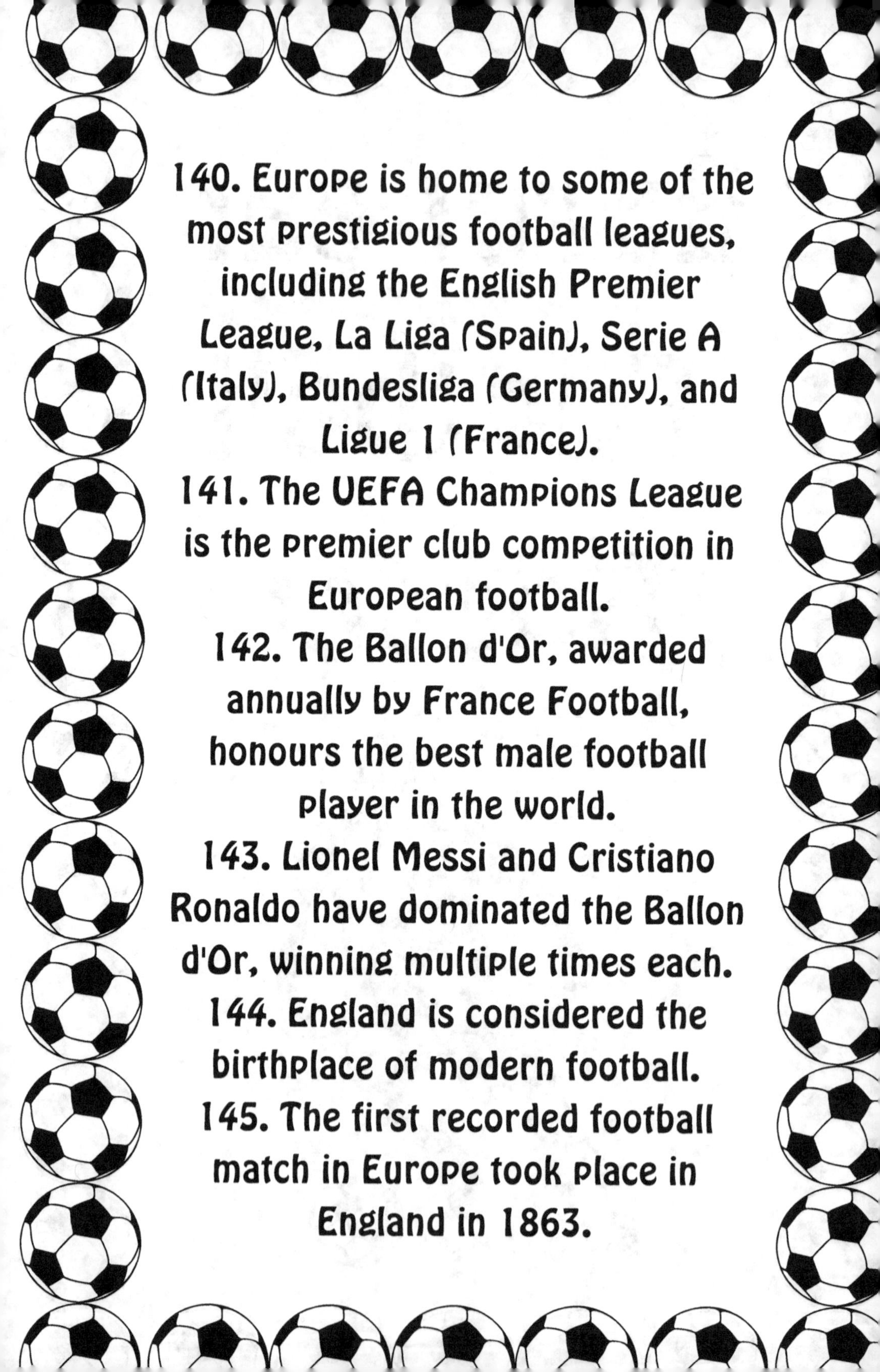

140. Europe is home to some of the most prestigious football leagues, including the English Premier League, La Liga (Spain), Serie A (Italy), Bundesliga (Germany), and Ligue 1 (France).

141. The UEFA Champions League is the premier club competition in European football.

142. The Ballon d'Or, awarded annually by France Football, honours the best male football player in the world.

143. Lionel Messi and Cristiano Ronaldo have dominated the Ballon d'Or, winning multiple times each.

144. England is considered the birthplace of modern football.

145. The first recorded football match in Europe took place in England in 1863.

146. The European Championship (Euro) is the quadrennial national team competition in Europe.

147. The most successful club in UEFA Champions League history is Real Madrid, with 13 titles.

148. The oldest football club in Europe is Sheffield FC, founded in 1857 in England.

149. The first recorded football match in Europe took place in England in 1863.

150. The first international football match in Europe was played between England and Scotland in 1872.

151. The Scottish Football Association is the world's oldest national football association, founded in 1873.

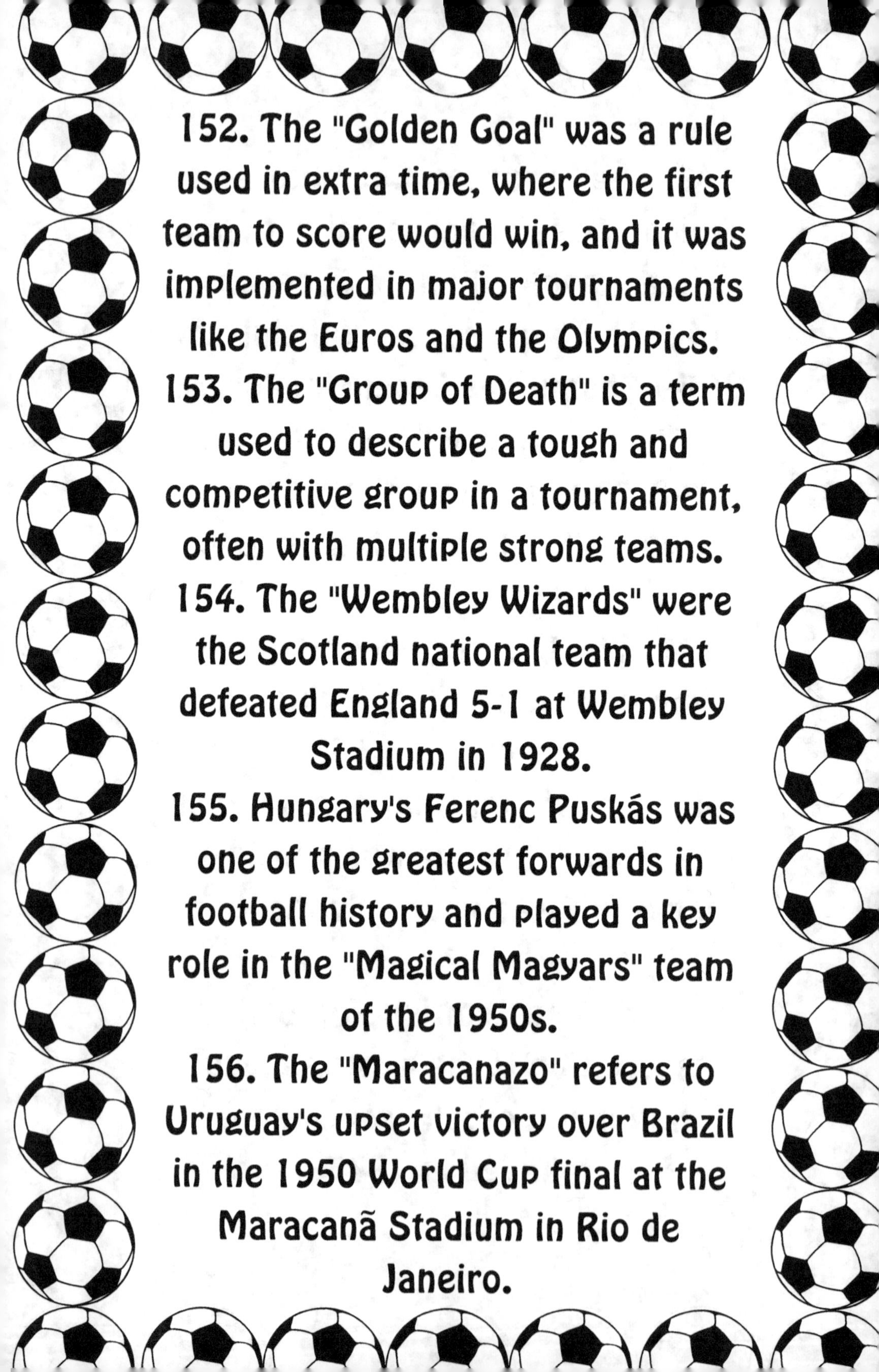

152. The "Golden Goal" was a rule used in extra time, where the first team to score would win, and it was implemented in major tournaments like the Euros and the Olympics.

153. The "Group of Death" is a term used to describe a tough and competitive group in a tournament, often with multiple strong teams.

154. The "Wembley Wizards" were the Scotland national team that defeated England 5-1 at Wembley Stadium in 1928.

155. Hungary's Ferenc Puskás was one of the greatest forwards in football history and played a key role in the "Magical Magyars" team of the 1950s.

156. The "Maracanazo" refers to Uruguay's upset victory over Brazil in the 1950 World Cup final at the Maracanã Stadium in Rio de Janeiro.

157. The 1954 World Cup final between Hungary and West Germany is known as the "Miracle of Bern," with West Germany coming from 2-0 down to win 3-2.
158. The "Busby Babes" were the young and talented Manchester United team managed by Matt Busby, tragically affected by the Munich air disaster in 1958.
159. The "Leeds Salute" is a celebration popularized by Leeds United fans during the 1960s.
160. The 1960 European Championship was the first-ever edition and was won by the Soviet Union.
161. The "Great Inter" team in the 1960s, led by Helenio Herrera, won three consecutive European Cups.

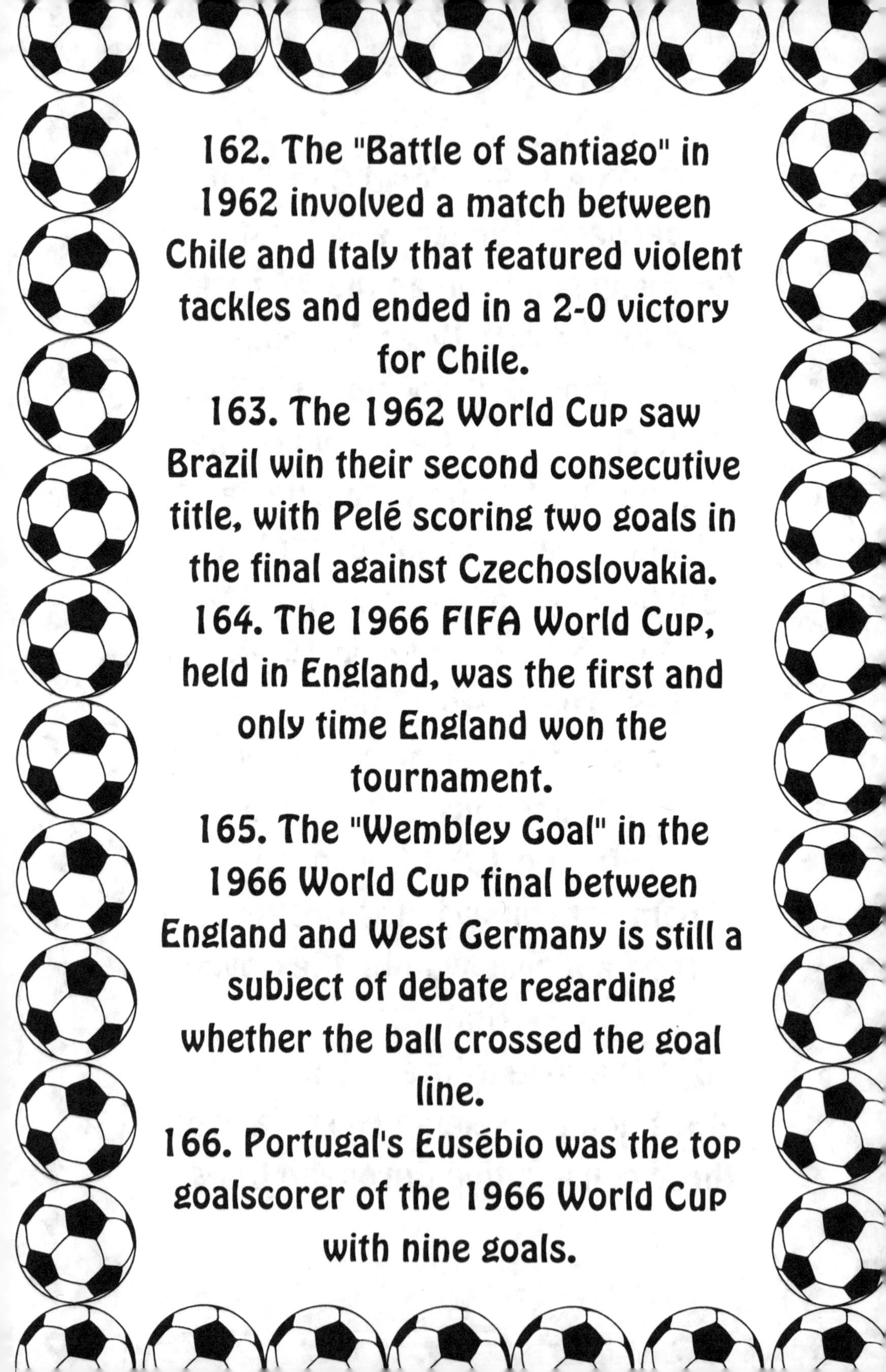

162. The "Battle of Santiago" in 1962 involved a match between Chile and Italy that featured violent tackles and ended in a 2-0 victory for Chile.

163. The 1962 World Cup saw Brazil win their second consecutive title, with Pelé scoring two goals in the final against Czechoslovakia.

164. The 1966 FIFA World Cup, held in England, was the first and only time England won the tournament.

165. The "Wembley Goal" in the 1966 World Cup final between England and West Germany is still a subject of debate regarding whether the ball crossed the goal line.

166. Portugal's Eusébio was the top goalscorer of the 1966 World Cup with nine goals.

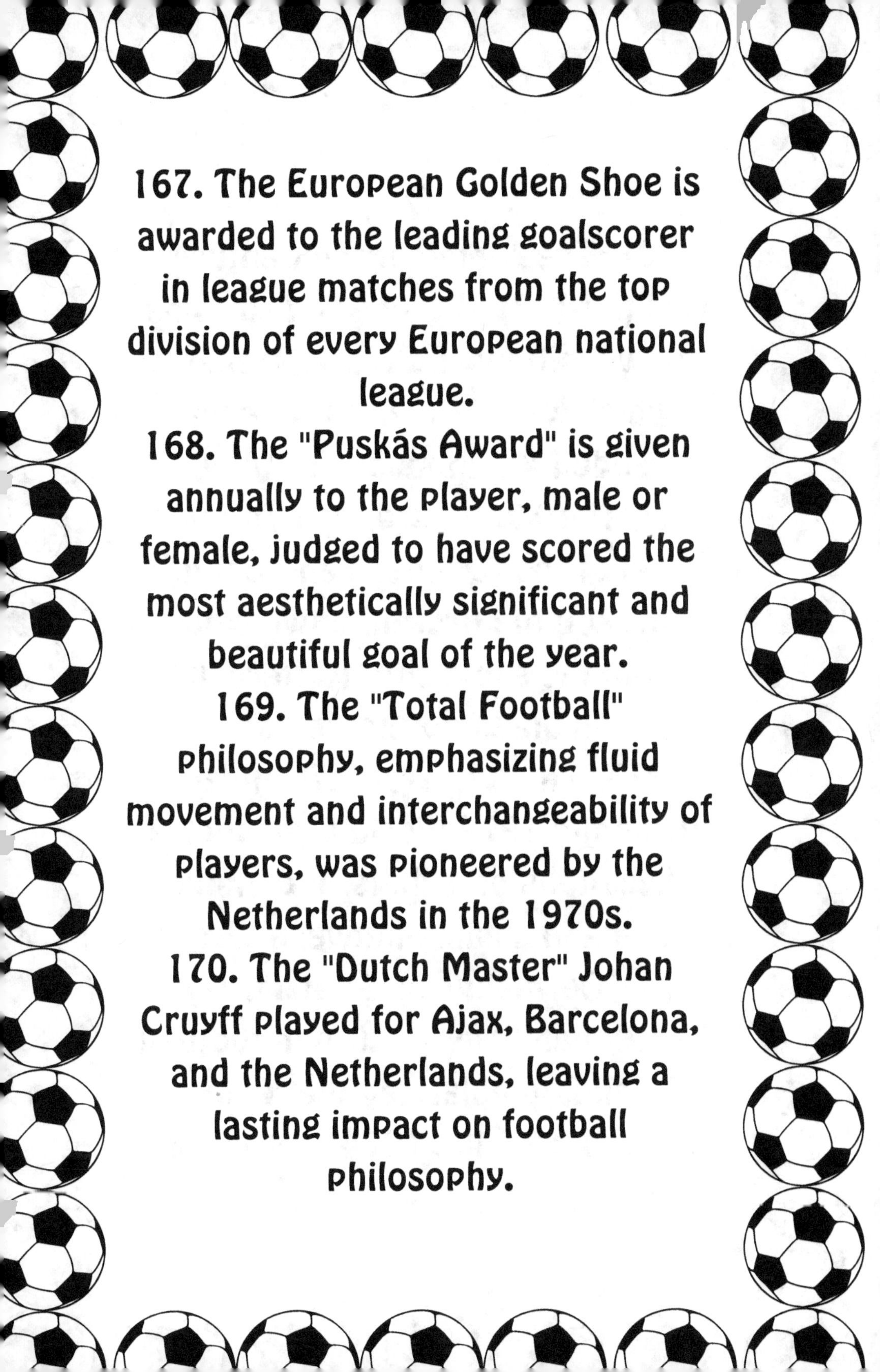

167. The European Golden Shoe is awarded to the leading goalscorer in league matches from the top division of every European national league.

168. The "Puskás Award" is given annually to the player, male or female, judged to have scored the most aesthetically significant and beautiful goal of the year.

169. The "Total Football" philosophy, emphasizing fluid movement and interchangeability of players, was pioneered by the Netherlands in the 1970s.

170. The "Dutch Master" Johan Cruyff played for Ajax, Barcelona, and the Netherlands, leaving a lasting impact on football philosophy.

171. The "Game of the Century" was the 1970 World Cup semi-final between Italy and West Germany, which went into extra time and ended 4-3 in favour of Italy.
172. The 1970 European Cup final between Feyenoord and Celtic marked the first time two clubs from the same city (Rotterdam) contested the final.
173. The "Watergate Scandal" during the 1974 World Cup involved allegations of bribery and match-fixing in a game between West Germany and Austria.
174. Johan Cruyff, a Dutch football legend, popularized the "Cruyff Turn" during the 1974 World Cup.

175. The "Panenka" penalty, a cheeky chip down the middle, was first successfully executed by Czechoslovakia's Antonín Panenka in the 1976 European Championship final.

176. The 1976 European Championship final between Czechoslovakia and West Germany was decided by a penalty shootout, with Czechoslovakia winning.

177. The "Miracle of Cordoba" refers to Austria defeating West Germany in the final match of the 1978 World Cup group stage.

178. The 1980 European Championship final featured West Germany defeating Belgium to win the title.

179. The 1982 World Cup featured one of the greatest matches in history, known as the "Match of the Century," where West Germany defeated France 5-4 in a penalty shootout after a 3-3 draw.

180. The 1984 European Championship final featured Michel Platini scoring nine goals in the tournament, leading France to victory.

181. The "Hand of God" goal, famously scored by Diego Maradona in the 1986 World Cup, was against England in the quarter-finals.

182. The 1988 European Championship final between the Netherlands and the Soviet Union was won by the Dutch, with Marco van Basten scoring a memorable goal.

183. The 1990 World Cup semi-final between West Germany and England ended with a penalty shootout, famously remembered for Andreas Brehme's decisive goal.

184. The 1992 European Championship marked the first time the tournament included a unified Germany.

185. The "Battle of Old Trafford" in 1994 was a Premier League match between Manchester United and Arsenal, marred by a physical altercation between players.

186. The 1994 World Cup in the United States was the first held outside of Europe and South America

187. The "Bosman ruling" in 1995 revolutionized football transfers by allowing players to move freely at the end of their contracts.

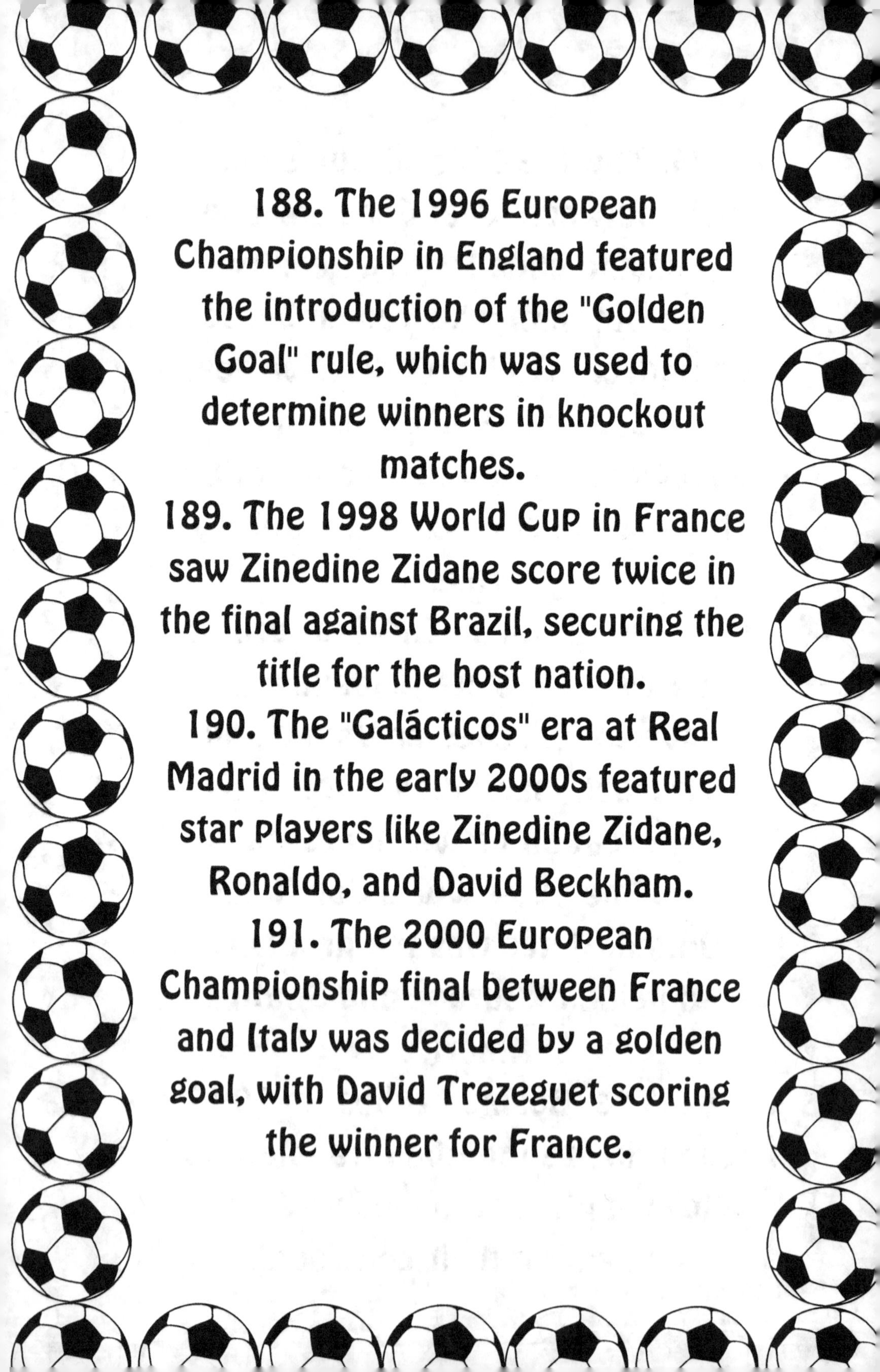

188. The 1996 European Championship in England featured the introduction of the "Golden Goal" rule, which was used to determine winners in knockout matches.

189. The 1998 World Cup in France saw Zinedine Zidane score twice in the final against Brazil, securing the title for the host nation.

190. The "Galácticos" era at Real Madrid in the early 2000s featured star players like Zinedine Zidane, Ronaldo, and David Beckham.

191. The 2000 European Championship final between France and Italy was decided by a golden goal, with David Trezeguet scoring the winner for France.

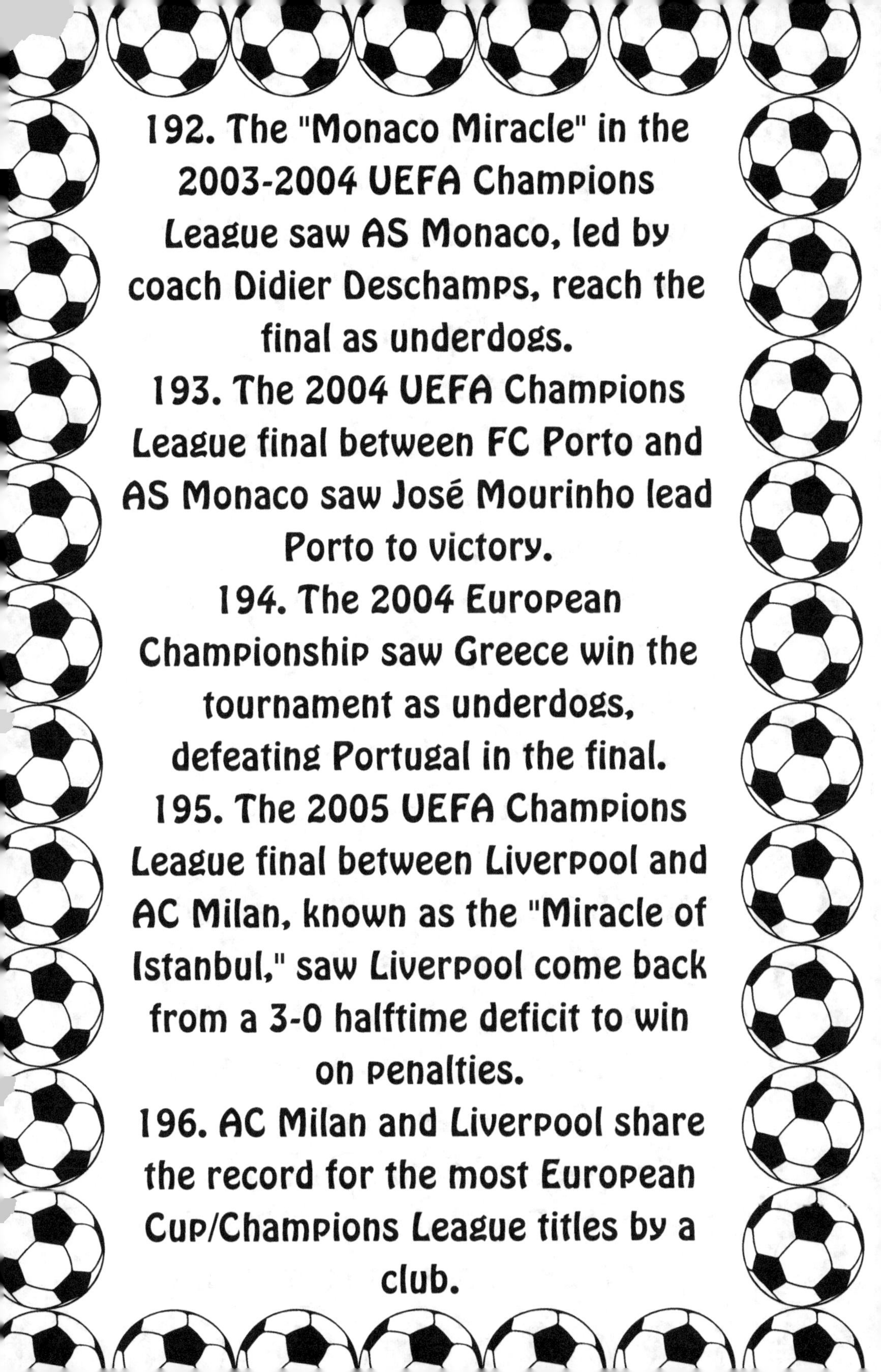

192. The "Monaco Miracle" in the 2003-2004 UEFA Champions League saw AS Monaco, led by coach Didier Deschamps, reach the final as underdogs.

193. The 2004 UEFA Champions League final between FC Porto and AS Monaco saw José Mourinho lead Porto to victory.

194. The 2004 European Championship saw Greece win the tournament as underdogs, defeating Portugal in the final.

195. The 2005 UEFA Champions League final between Liverpool and AC Milan, known as the "Miracle of Istanbul," saw Liverpool come back from a 3-0 halftime deficit to win on penalties.

196. AC Milan and Liverpool share the record for the most European Cup/Champions League titles by a club.

197. The "Catenaccio" system, characterized by a strong defence, was popularized by Italian clubs, notably Helenio Herrera's Inter Milan.

198. The 2006 World Cup final between Italy and France ended in a penalty shootout, with Italy emerging as the champions.

199. The "Battle of Nuremberg" during the 2006 World Cup featured a match between Portugal and the Netherlands that saw a record four red cards and 16 yellow cards.

200. The "Sausage Roll" celebration became popular after Peter Crouch scored for England in the 2006 World Cup, imitating a robot dance.

201. The fastest goal in UEFA Champions League history was scored by Roy Makaay in 2007, just 10.12 seconds into a match.

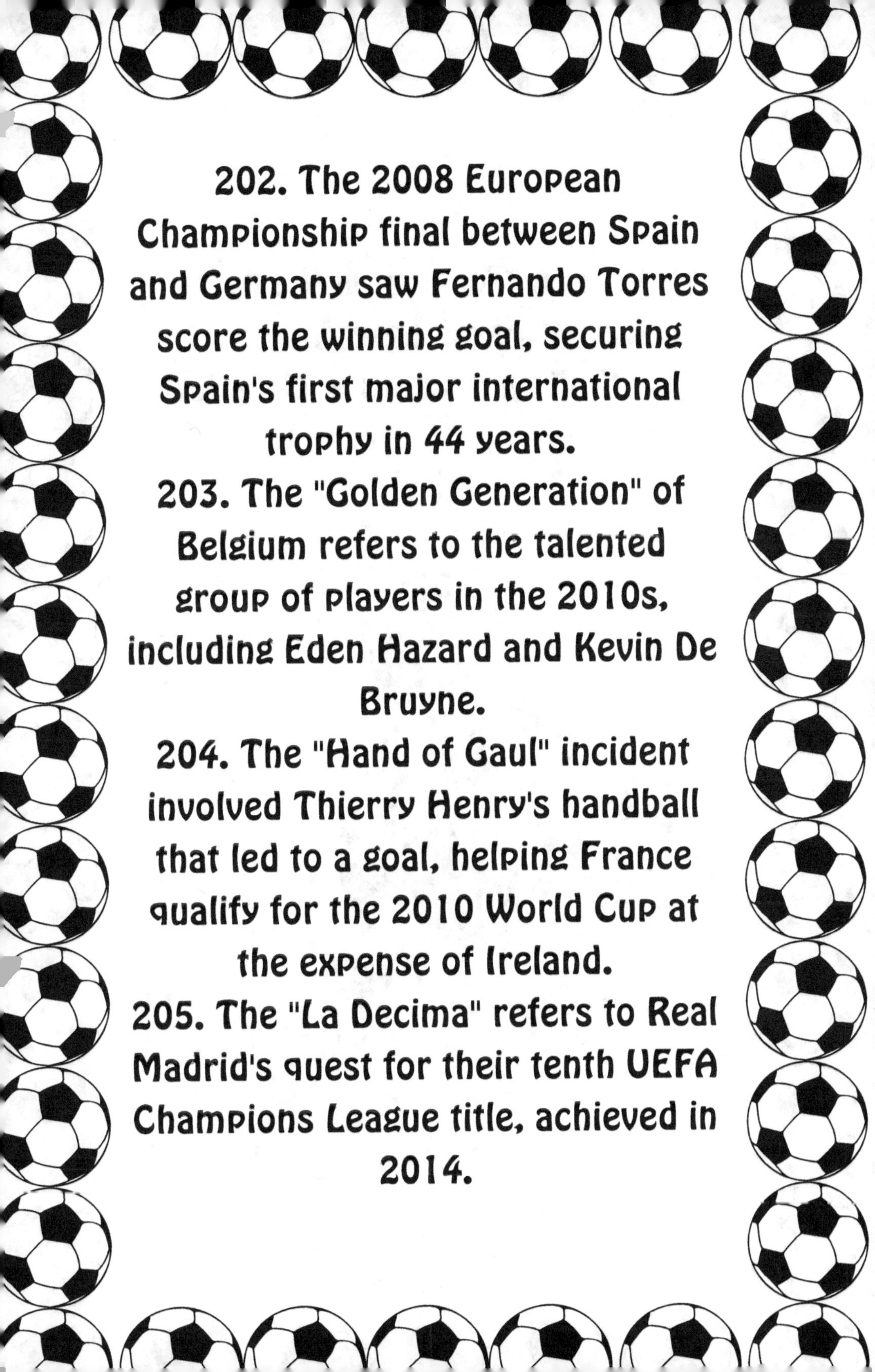

202. The 2008 European Championship final between Spain and Germany saw Fernando Torres score the winning goal, securing Spain's first major international trophy in 44 years.

203. The "Golden Generation" of Belgium refers to the talented group of players in the 2010s, including Eden Hazard and Kevin De Bruyne.

204. The "Hand of Gaul" incident involved Thierry Henry's handball that led to a goal, helping France qualify for the 2010 World Cup at the expense of Ireland.

205. The "La Decima" refers to Real Madrid's quest for their tenth UEFA Champions League title, achieved in 2014.

206. The "Torcida" is the name given to passionate and vocal football supporters in Croatia.

Basketball

207. Basketball was invented by Dr. James Naismith in December 1891 in Springfield, Massachusetts.

208. The first official game of women's basketball was played at Smith College in 1893.

209. The first official game of basketball was played with a soccer ball and two peach baskets as goals.

210. The National Basketball Association (NBA) is the premier professional basketball league in the world.

211. The EuroLeague is the top-tier professional basketball league in Europe.

212. The NBA's logo features the silhouette of Jerry West, a Hall of Fame player.

213. The first basketball game in the Olympics was played in 1936.

214. The NBA's Sacramento Kings were originally known as the Rochester Royals and were one of the league's founding members.

215. The Harlem Globetrotters, known for their entertaining and skilled basketball performances, were founded in 1926.

216. The Harlem Globetrotters have played exhibition games in over 120 countries.

217. The first NBA game was played on November 1, 1946, between the New York Knicks and the Toronto Huskies.

218. The first official game of wheelchair basketball was played in 1946 in the United States.

219. The 24-second shot clock was introduced to the NBA in 1954 to speed up the pace of the game.

220. The first NBA player to score a triple-double (double-digit stats in three categories) was Maurice Stokes in 1955.

221. The "Triple-Double" refers to a player recording double-digit stats in three categories, typically points, rebounds, and assists.

222. The NBA's Detroit Pistons were originally the Fort Wayne Pistons before relocating in 1957.

223. The NBA's Golden State Warriors were originally the Philadelphia Warriors before relocating in 1962.

224. The NBA's Philadelphia 76ers were originally the Syracuse Nationals before relocating in 1963.

225. The NBA's Milwaukee Bucks were one of two expansion teams added in 1968.

226. The NBA's Portland Trail Blazers were one of two expansion teams added in 1970, along with the Cleveland Cavaliers

227. The NBA's Los Angeles Clippers were originally the Buffalo Braves before relocating in 1978.

228. The NBA's Utah Jazz were originally the New Orleans Jazz before relocating in 1979.

229. The NBA Draft Lottery was first introduced in 1985 to determine the order of selection for teams in the draft.

230. The NBA's Miami Heat and the Charlotte Bobcats were added as expansion teams in 1988.

231. The NBA's Charlotte Hornets were initially an expansion team in 1988, later moving to New Orleans before returning to Charlotte in 2004.

232. The Chicago Bulls achieved two three-peats (three consecutive championships) in the 1990s with Michael Jordan.

233. The "Fab Five" refers to the University of Michigan's men's basketball team in the early 1990s, known for their baggy shorts and cultural impact.

234. The "Dream Team" was the U.S. men's basketball team that dominated the 1992 Barcelona Olympics, featuring players like Michael Jordan, Magic Johnson, and Larry Bird.

235. Michael Jordan is widely considered one of the greatest basketball players of all time.

236. The "Dream Team II" was the U.S. men's basketball team that won the gold medal at the 1994 FIBA World Championship.

237. The tallest NBA player ever was Gheorghe Mureșan, standing at 7 feet 7 inches tall.

238. The shortest player in NBA history is Tyrone "Muggsy" Bogues, who is 5 feet 3 inches tall.

239. The NCAA Women's Basketball Tournament expanded to 64 teams in 1994.

240. The WNBA was founded in 1996, with the Houston Comets winning the first championship.

241. The NBA's Orlando Magic and the Toronto Raptors were the first teams to play regular-season games in Japan in 1996.

242. The WNBA's New York Liberty was one of the league's eight original franchises in 1997.

243. The San Antonio Spurs have had a remarkable run of success, making the NBA playoffs for 22 consecutive seasons from 1998 to 2019.

244. The NBA's Memphis Grizzlies were originally the Vancouver Grizzlies before relocating in 2001.

245. Lisa Leslie became the first woman to dunk in a WNBA game in 2002.

246. The WNBA's Las Vegas Aces were originally the Utah Starzz before relocating in 2003.

247. The WNBA's Phoenix Mercury and the Detroit Shock played in the longest game in league history, lasting three overtimes in 2007.

248. The NBA's Oklahoma City Thunder were initially the Seattle SuperSonics before relocating in 2008.

249. The first official basketball game played outdoors in the NBA occurred in 2008 at the Indian Wells Tennis Garden in California.

250. The Boston Celtics have won the most NBA championships, with 17 titles.

251. The WNBA's Atlanta Dream was one of three expansion teams added in 2008.

252. The WNBA's Dallas Wings were originally the Detroit Shock before relocating in 2010.

253. The Chicago Bulls' Derrick Rose became the youngest player to win the NBA Most Valuable Player (MVP) award in 2011.

254. The WNBA's Minnesota Lynx won four championships in seven years (2011, 2013, 2015, 2017).

255. The NBA's Brooklyn Nets were originally the New Jersey Nets before relocating in 2012.

256. The WNBA's Indiana Fever won their first championship in 2012.

257. The NBA's New Orleans Pelicans were initially the New Orleans Hornets before changing their name in 2013.

258. The NBA's Golden State Warriors set a regular-season record with 73 wins in the 2015-2016 season.

259. The WNBA's Los Angeles Sparks and the Minnesota Lynx played in the first WNBA Finals to go to a decisive fifth game in 2016.

260. The NBA's Toronto Raptors won their first NBA championship in 2019, led by Finals MVP Kawhi Leonard.

261. The NBA's Miami Heat became the first team to reach the NBA Finals from the eighth seed in 2020.

262. The Phoenix Suns and the Milwaukee Bucks faced off in the first NBA Finals held in July, as the league adjusted its schedule due to the COVID-19 pandemic in 2021.

263. The WNBA's Chicago Sky won their first championship in 2021.

264. The NBA Finals MVP award is named after Bill Russell, one of the greatest players in NBA history.

265. The NCAA Men's Basketball Tournament, known as March Madness, is a single-elimination tournament held annually in the United States.

266. Kareem Abdul-Jabbar is the NBA's all-time leading scorer, with 38,387 points.

267. The "Skyhook" shot, perfected by Kareem Abdul-Jabbar, is one of the most effective, iconic, and difficult-to-defend moves in basketball.

268. The first African-American head coach in the NBA was Bill Russell, who also served as a player-coach for the Boston Celtics.

269.The Phoenix Suns' Gorilla and the Utah Jazz's Bear are two popular NBA mascots known for their entertaining antics.

270. Hakeem Olajuwon is the only player in NBA history to record over 200 blocks and 200 steals in a single season.

271. The "Hack-a-Shaq" strategy, intentionally fouling a poor free-throw shooter like Shaquille O'Neal, became a popular tactic in the NBA.

272. The NBA's "One-and-Done" rule requires players to be at least 19 years old and one year removed from high school before entering the draft.

273. The "Pistol" Pete Maravich is one of the greatest college basketball players in history, holding numerous scoring records.

274. The Dallas Mavericks' Dirk Nowitzki, a German player, revolutionized the game as one of the best-shooting big men in NBA history.

275. The WNBA's Seattle Storm and the Houston Comets are tied for the most championships in the league, with four each.

276. The "EuroStep," a deceptive sidestep move, was popularized by European players like Manu Ginóbili.

277. The NBA's Washington Wizards were originally the Chicago Packers before becoming the Chicago Zephyrs and then the Baltimore Bullets.

278. The "Black Mamba" was the nickname of the late Kobe Bryant, one of the greatest players in NBA history.

279. The NBA's Atlanta Hawks were originally the Buffalo Bisons and later became the Tri-Cities Blackhawks.

280. The "Shammgod" dribble move, popularized by God Shammgod, is a deceptive way to change direction with the ball.

281. The "Dream Shake" was a signature move of Hakeem Olajuwon, involving a series of fakes and pivots to create space for a shot.

282. The NBA's New York Knicks play their home games at Madison Square Garden, often referred to as "The Mecca of Basketball."

283. The "Four-Point Play" occurs when a player makes a three-point shot and is fouled, earning a free throw.

284. The "Dribble-Drive Motion Offense" emphasizes penetration and kick-out passes to create open shots.

285. The "Elam Ending" is a format where teams play to a target score instead of a fixed game time, introduced in the NBA All-Star Game

286. The "Nellie Ball" style of play is named after coach Don Nelson, known for his innovative and up-tempo strategies.

287. The "And-1 Mixtape Tour" showcased streetball players performing flashy and unconventional moves.

Baseball

288. Baseball is often referred to as "America's Pastime."

289. The first recorded baseball game in history took place in Hoboken, New Jersey, in 1846.

290. Abner Doubleday is often erroneously credited with inventing baseball, but there is no evidence to support this claim.

291. The Cincinnati Reds were the first professional baseball team, established in 1869.

292. The first official game of softball was played indoors in 1887, using a broomstick and a rolled-up boxing glove.

293. The "Tinker to Evers to Chance" double-play combination for the Chicago Cubs in the early 20th century was immortalized in a famous poem.

294. The "Pittsburgh Lumber Company" referred to the powerful hitting lineup of the Pittsburgh Pirates in the early 20th century.

295. The "Dead-Ball Era" in baseball refers to the period from the early 1900s to the 1920s when offense was limited, and balls were not replaced frequently.

296. "Take Me Out to the Ball Game" is a famous baseball song written in 1908 by Jack Norworth and Albert Von Tilzer.

297 The oldest major league baseball park still in use is Fenway Park, home of the Boston Red Sox, which opened in 1912.

298. The "Curse of the Bambino" refers to the superstition that the Boston Red Sox were cursed after trading Babe Ruth to the New York Yankees in 1919.

299. The "Chicago Black Sox Scandal" involved members of the 1919 Chicago White Sox intentionally losing the World Series in exchange for money from gamblers.

300. The "Babe Ruth Home Run Call Shot" incident in the 1932 World Series involves Ruth allegedly pointing to the center-field bleachers before hitting a home run.

301. The "Gashouse Gang" was the nickname for the 1934 St. Louis Cardinals, known for their scrappy and unorthodox style of play.

302. The "Duffy's Cliff" was a steep incline in left field at Boston's Fenway Park before it was levelled in 1934.

303. Jackie Robinson broke the colour barrier in baseball when he debuted for the Brooklyn Dodgers in 1947.

304. The "Bonus Baby" rule in the 1950s allowed teams to sign high school players to big league contracts, leading to increased pressure on young players.

305. The "Shot Heard 'Round the World" was Bobby Thomson's game-winning home run in 1951, securing the New York Giants' National League pennant.

306. The "Los Angeles Dodgers" were originally the Brooklyn Dodgers before relocating in 1958.

307. The shortest nine-inning perfect game in MLB history was pitched by Harvey Haddix in 1959, but he lost the game in extra innings.

308. The "AstroTurf" artificial playing surface was first used in baseball in the late 1960s.

314. Babe Ruth, known as "The Sultan of Swat," held the home run record with 714 until it was surpassed by Hank Aaron.

315. The "Fernandomania" craze swept through baseball in 1981 when Fernando Valenzuela, a rookie pitcher for the Los Angeles Dodgers, became a sensation.

316. The longest professional baseball game lasted 33 innings and took place in 1981 between the Pawtucket Red Sox and the Rochester Red Wings.

317. The "Fog Game" took place in 1982 between the Chicago White Sox and Milwaukee Brewers, with fog making it challenging to see the action.

318. The "Pine Tar Incident" in 1983 involved George Brett's home run being nullified due to excessive pine tar on his bat.

319. The "Fog Bowl" in 1988 involved a playoff game between the Chicago Bears and the Philadelphia Eagles played in dense fog.

320. The "Field of Dreams" is a famous baseball movie released in 1989, starring Kevin Costner and Ray Liotta.

321. The "Baby Braves" were the young and talented Atlanta Braves teams of the late 1990s and early 2000s.

322. The "Killer B's" were a trio of Houston Astros players in the late 1990s – Jeff Bagwell, Craig Biggio, and Derek Bell

323. "The Sandlot" is a popular baseball movie released in 1993, depicting the adventures of a group of young baseball players.

324. The baseball field is sometimes called a "diamond" due to its shape.

325. The "Grand Slam Single" took place in the 1999 National League Championship Series when Robin Ventura hit a grand slam, but the game ended on the basepaths before he reached second base.

326. The "Gyroball" is a mythical and controversial pitch that was said to defy the laws of physics, attracting attention in the early 2000s.

327. The "Rally Monkey" became a symbol of good luck for the Anaheim Angels during their 2002 World Series run.

328. The "Four Aces" referred to the dominant pitching rotation of the 2011 Philadelphia Phillies.

329. The "Bullpen Mafia" was a term used to describe the dominant bullpen of the 2014 Kansas City Royals

330. The "Chicago Cubs Curse" was broken in 2016 when the team won the World Series for the first time in 108 years.

331. The baseball field is sometimes called a "diamond" due to its shape.

332. The distance between bases on a baseball field is 90 feet.

333. A regulation baseball game consists of nine innings.

334. The New York Yankees have won the most World Series championships, with 27 titles.

335. The longest professional baseball game lasted 33 innings and took place in 1981 between the Pawtucket Red Sox and the Rochester Red Wings.

336. Baseballs used in the major leagues are made with cowhide and have 108 stitches.

337. The "Mendoza Line" is a term used to describe a batting average of .200, named after Mario Mendoza, a player known for his low batting average.

338. The Cy Young Award is given annually to the best pitchers in Major League Baseball.

339. The "Hidden Ball Trick" is a deceptive play where an infielder pretends to return the ball to the pitcher but keeps it instead, waiting for a baserunner to step off the base.

340. The New York Yankees and the Boston Red Sox have one of the most intense and historic rivalries in baseball.

341. The "Immaculate Inning" is when a pitcher strikes out all three batters in a half-inning on just nine pitches.

342. The "Perfect Game" is a game in which a pitcher faces 27 batters and none of them reach base.

343. The "Green Monster" is the nickname for the left-field wall at Fenway Park, known for its height and impact on the game.
Baseball Hall of Famer Nolan Ryan holds the record for the most career strikeouts, with 5,714.
344. A "Cycle" in baseball is when a batter hits a single, double, triple, and home run in the same game.
345. The "Say Hey Kid" is the nickname for Hall of Famer Willie Mays.
346. The "L-Screen" is a protective screen used during batting practice to shield pitchers from line drives.
347. The "Brushback Pitch" is a high and inside pitch thrown close to a batter to make it uncomfortable in the batter's box.

348. The "Ted Williams Shift" is a defensive strategy where fielders shift to one side of the field to counter a hitter's tendencies.

349. The "Cooperstown" is a reference to the Baseball Hall of Fame, located in Cooperstown, New York.

350. "Take a Pitcher to Lunch" is a campaign initiated by baseball player Tug McGraw to honour pitchers for their contributions to the game.

351. The "Rain Shortened No-Hitter" is a rare occurrence where a pitcher throws a no-hitter, but the game is shortened due to rain.

352. The "Sweet Spot" on a baseball bat is the area where hitting the ball results in the least vibration and maximum power.

353. The "Black Aces" is a group of African American pitchers who have won at least 20 games in a single MLB season.

354. The "Baltimore Chop" is a hitting technique where a batter intentionally hits the ball into the ground to get a favourable bounce.

355. The "Wheelhouse" is the area of the strike zone where a batter has the most power and control.

356. The "Eephus Pitch" is a slow, high-arching pitch thrown with an unusual grip to surprise batters.

357. The "Hidden Ball Trick" is a deceptive play where an infielder hides the ball to catch a baserunner off guard.

358. The "Silver Slugger Award" is given to the best offensive players at each position in both the American and National Leagues.

359. The "Silver Boot Series" is an annual competition between the Texas Rangers and the Houston Astros for bragging rights in the state of Texas.

360. The "Tiger Stadium" in Detroit, Michigan, was known for its distinctive roofless upper deck and flagpole in the center field.

361. The "Mauer Power" chant became associated with Minnesota Twins fans cheering for Joe Mauer, a hometown player.

362. The "Baseball Rule 21" allows the commissioner to ban players involved in gambling or game-fixing.

363. The "Knothole Gang" refers to fans who watched games for free by peeking through knotholes in the outfield fence.

364. The "Cardinals Way" is a philosophy associated with the St. Louis Cardinals organization, emphasizing fundamentals and player development.

365. The "Baltimore Chop" is a hitting technique where a batter intentionally hits the ball into the ground to get a favourable bounce.

366. The "Eephus Pitch" is a slow, high-arching pitch thrown with an unusual grip to surprise batters.

367. The "Knuckleball" is a pitch with minimal spin, causing unpredictable movement and making it difficult for batters to hit.

368. The "No-Hitter" is a game in which a pitcher or a combination of pitchers prevents the opposing team from getting a hit.

367. The "Home Run Derby" is an annual event during the All-Star break where power hitters compete to hit the most home runs.

Motorsport

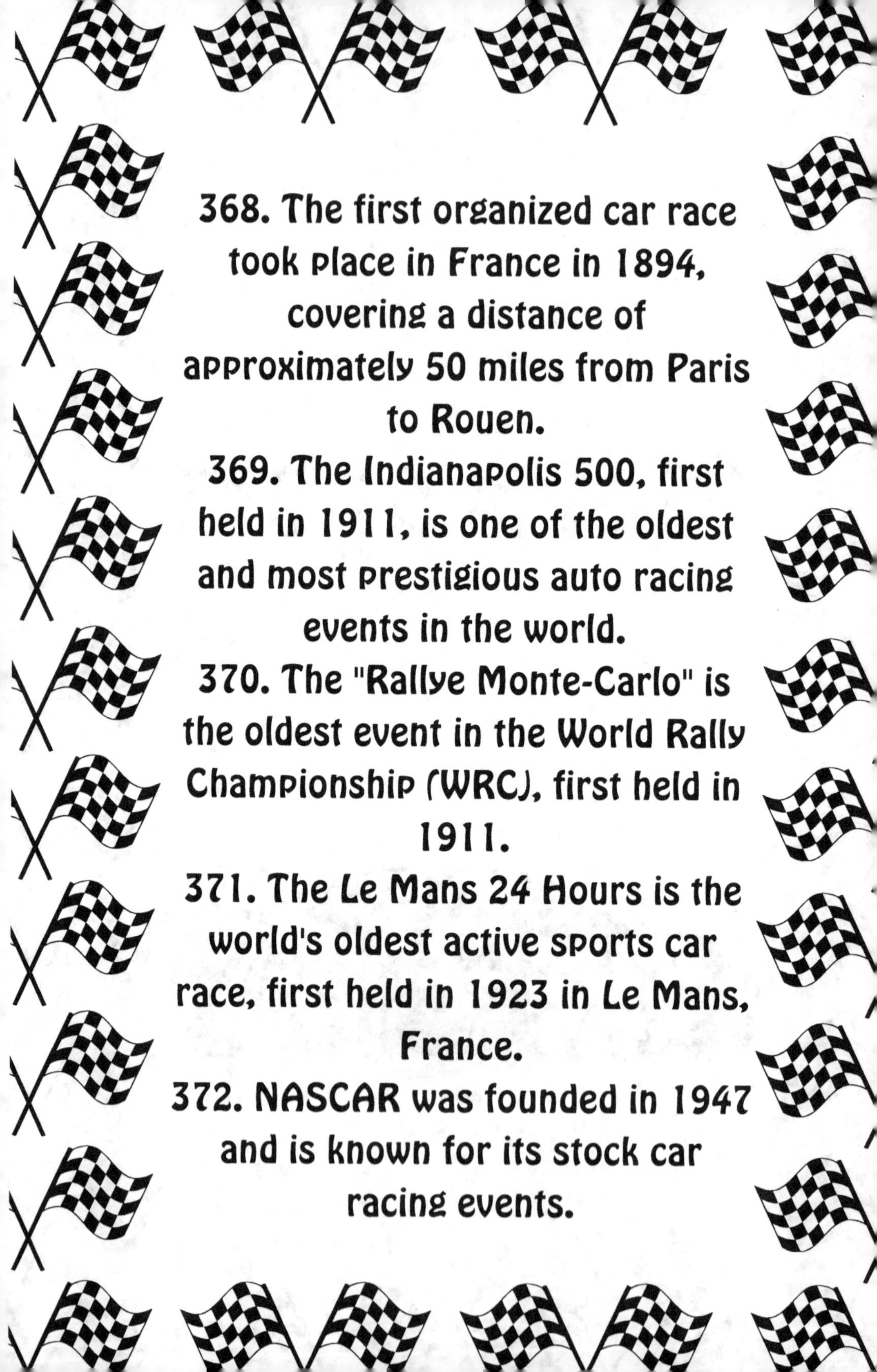

368. The first organized car race took place in France in 1894, covering a distance of approximately 50 miles from Paris to Rouen.

369. The Indianapolis 500, first held in 1911, is one of the oldest and most prestigious auto racing events in the world.

370. The "Rallye Monte-Carlo" is the oldest event in the World Rally Championship (WRC), first held in 1911.

371. The Le Mans 24 Hours is the world's oldest active sports car race, first held in 1923 in Le Mans, France.

372. NASCAR was founded in 1947 and is known for its stock car racing events.

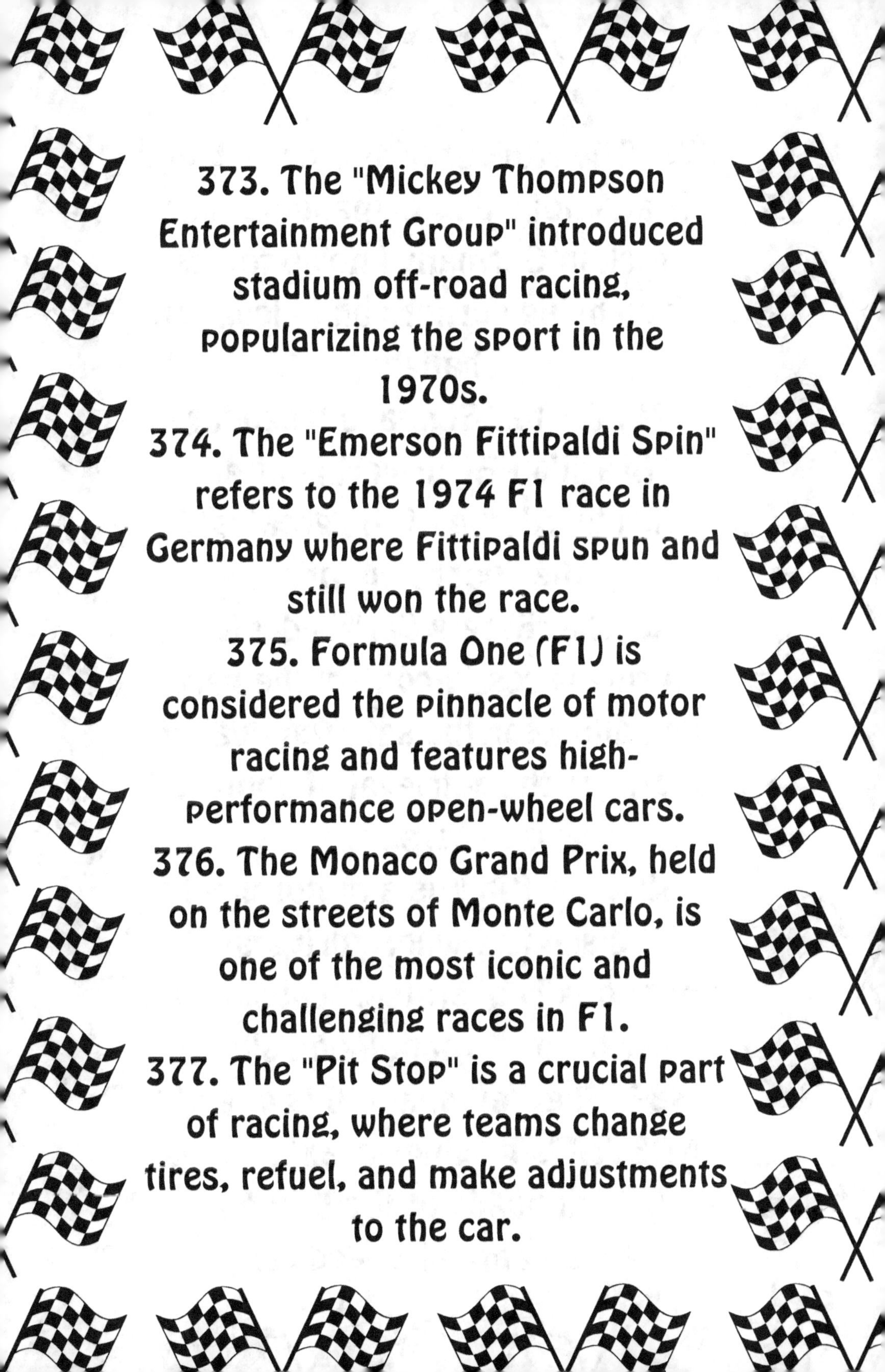

373. The "Mickey Thompson Entertainment Group" introduced stadium off-road racing, popularizing the sport in the 1970s.

374. The "Emerson Fittipaldi Spin" refers to the 1974 F1 race in Germany where Fittipaldi spun and still won the race.

375. Formula One (F1) is considered the pinnacle of motor racing and features high-performance open-wheel cars.

376. The Monaco Grand Prix, held on the streets of Monte Carlo, is one of the most iconic and challenging races in F1.

377. The "Pit Stop" is a crucial part of racing, where teams change tires, refuel, and make adjustments to the car.

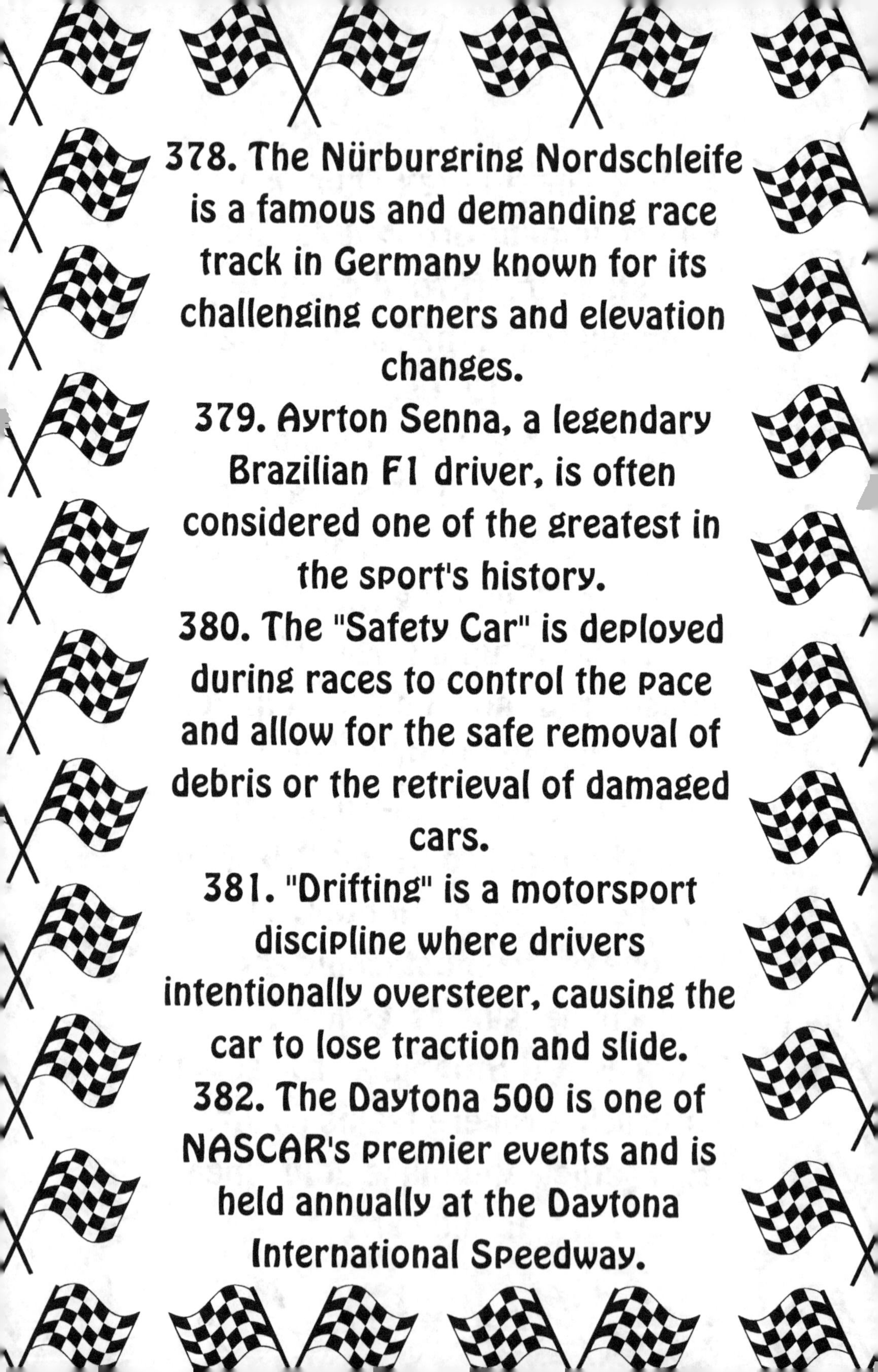

378. The Nürburgring Nordschleife is a famous and demanding race track in Germany known for its challenging corners and elevation changes.

379. Ayrton Senna, a legendary Brazilian F1 driver, is often considered one of the greatest in the sport's history.

380. The "Safety Car" is deployed during races to control the pace and allow for the safe removal of debris or the retrieval of damaged cars.

381. "Drifting" is a motorsport discipline where drivers intentionally oversteer, causing the car to lose traction and slide.

382. The Daytona 500 is one of NASCAR's premier events and is held annually at the Daytona International Speedway.

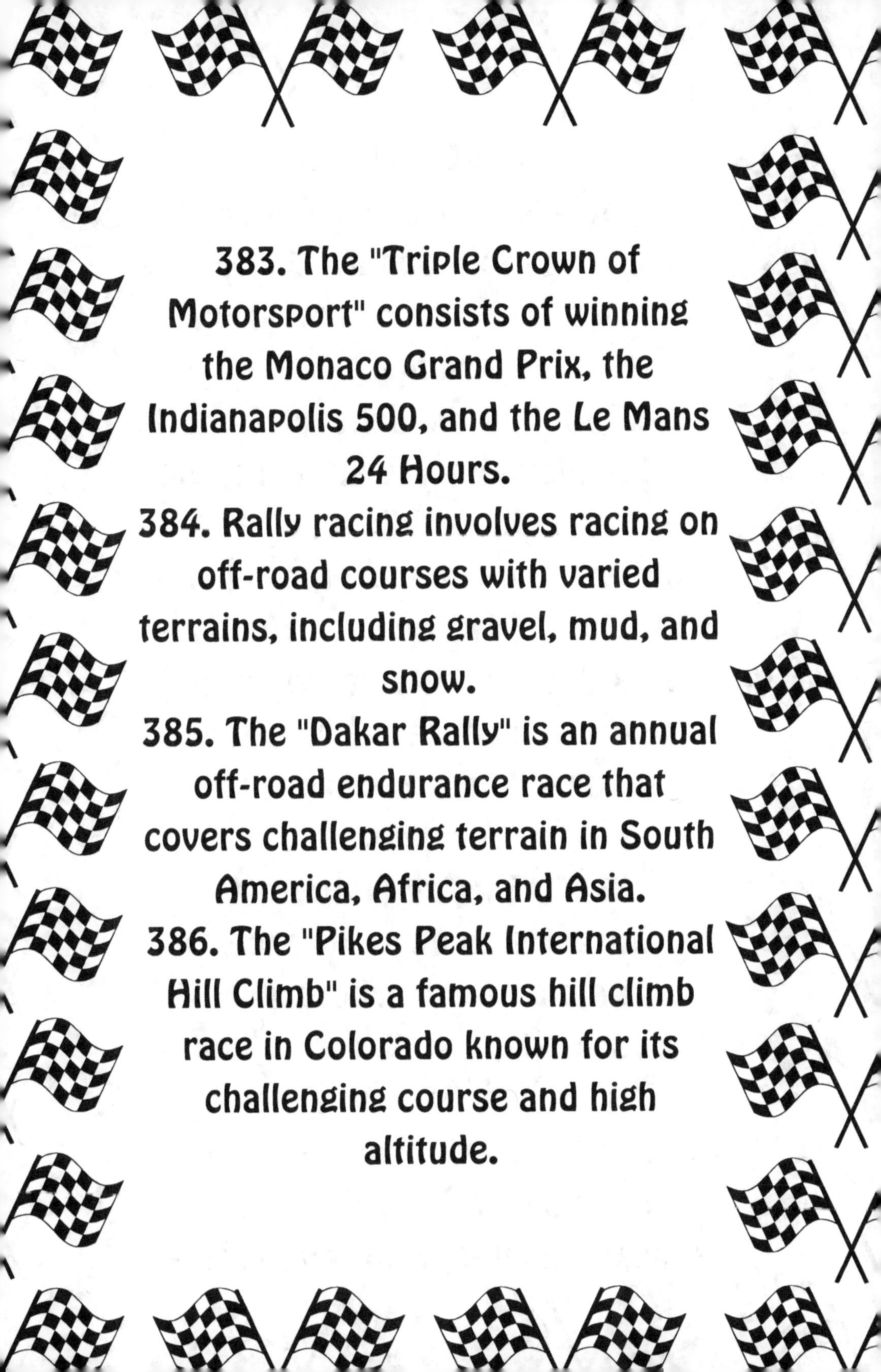

383. The "Triple Crown of Motorsport" consists of winning the Monaco Grand Prix, the Indianapolis 500, and the Le Mans 24 Hours.

384. Rally racing involves racing on off-road courses with varied terrains, including gravel, mud, and snow.

385. The "Dakar Rally" is an annual off-road endurance race that covers challenging terrain in South America, Africa, and Asia.

386. The "Pikes Peak International Hill Climb" is a famous hill climb race in Colorado known for its challenging course and high altitude.

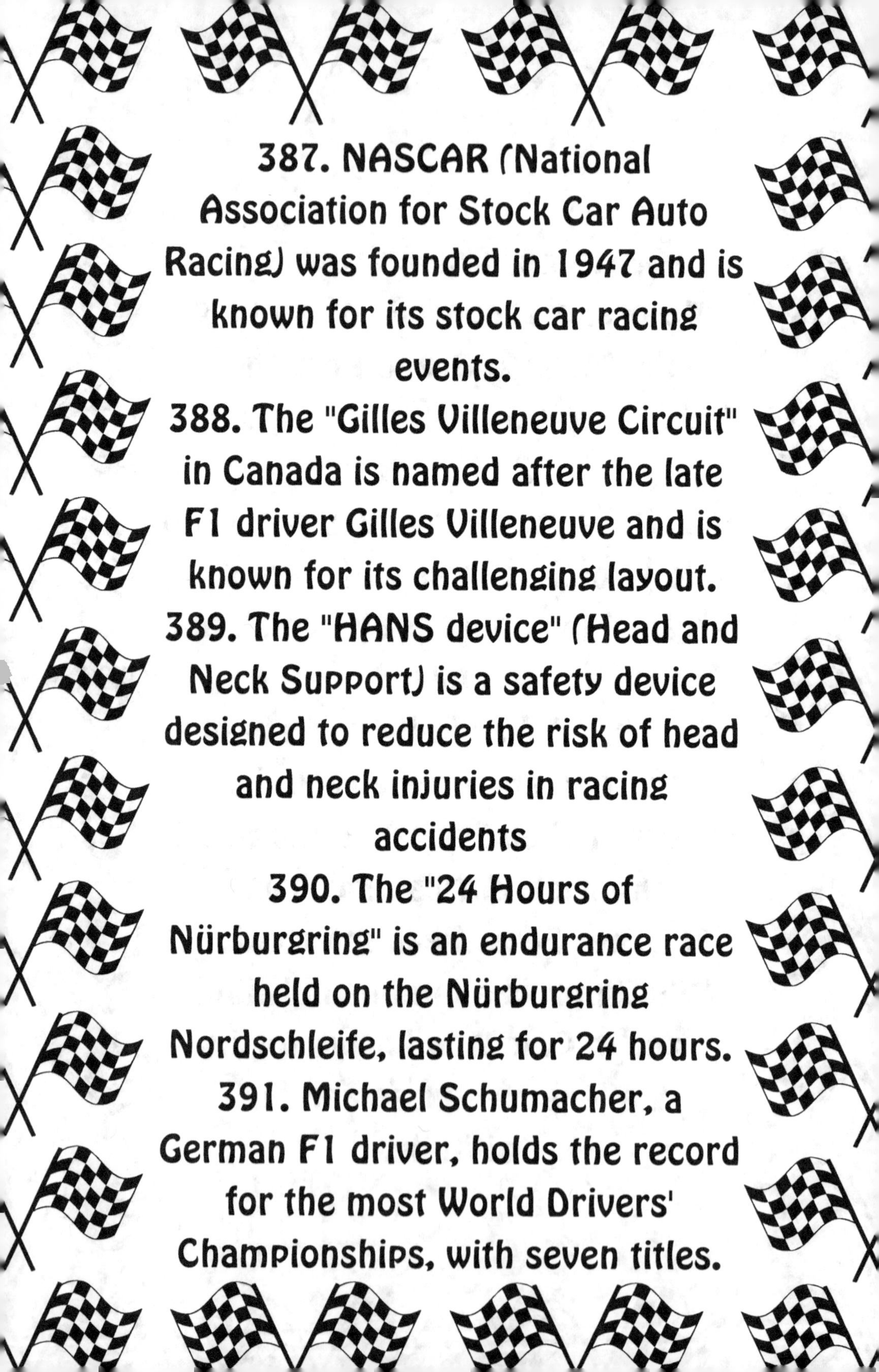

387. NASCAR (National Association for Stock Car Auto Racing) was founded in 1947 and is known for its stock car racing events.

388. The "Gilles Villeneuve Circuit" in Canada is named after the late F1 driver Gilles Villeneuve and is known for its challenging layout.

389. The "HANS device" (Head and Neck Support) is a safety device designed to reduce the risk of head and neck injuries in racing accidents

390. The "24 Hours of Nürburgring" is an endurance race held on the Nürburgring Nordschleife, lasting for 24 hours.

391. Michael Schumacher, a German F1 driver, holds the record for the most World Drivers' Championships, with seven titles.

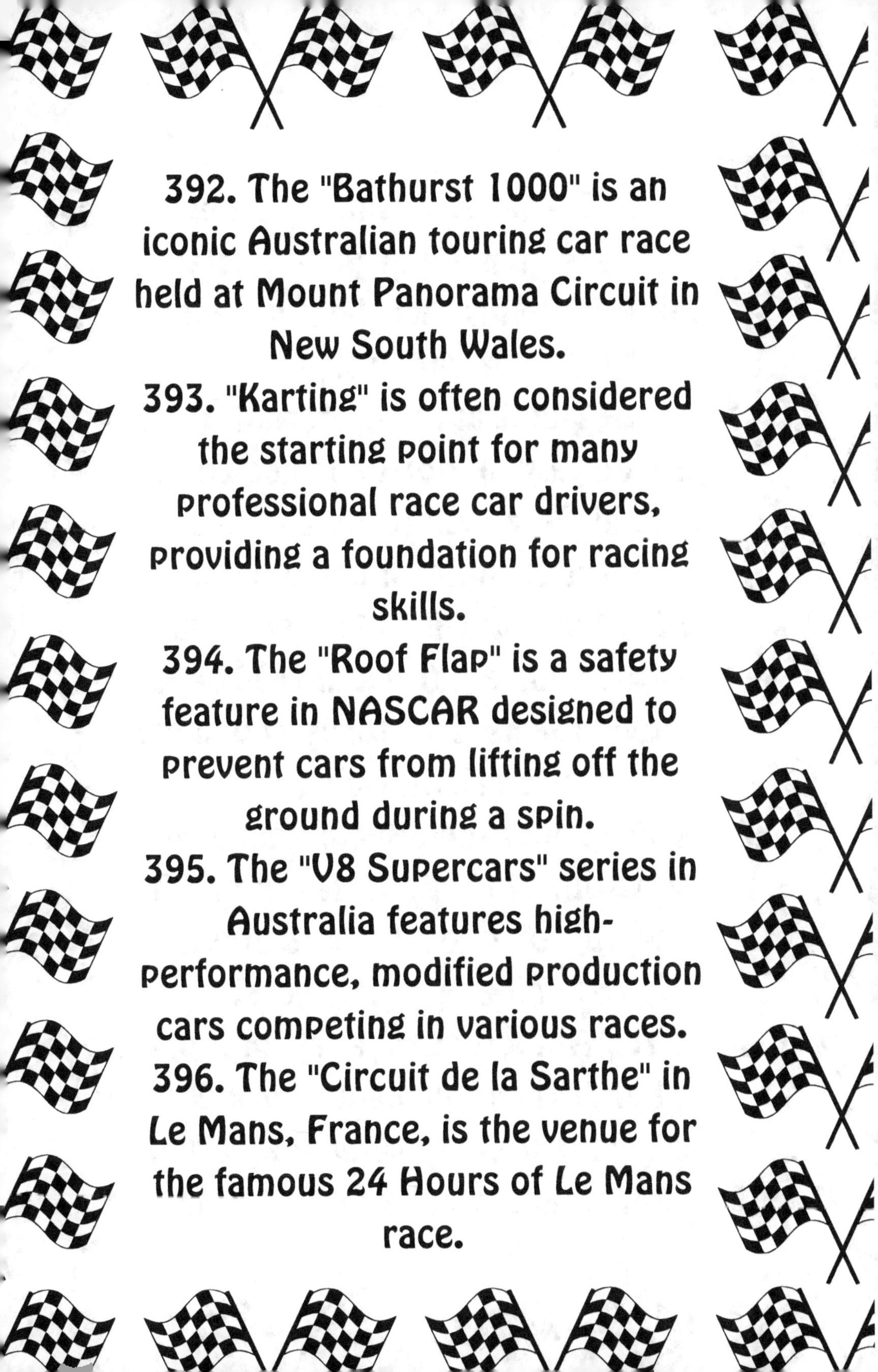

392. The "Bathurst 1000" is an iconic Australian touring car race held at Mount Panorama Circuit in New South Wales.

393. "Karting" is often considered the starting point for many professional race car drivers, providing a foundation for racing skills.

394. The "Roof Flap" is a safety feature in NASCAR designed to prevent cars from lifting off the ground during a spin.

395. The "V8 Supercars" series in Australia features high-performance, modified production cars competing in various races.

396. The "Circuit de la Sarthe" in Le Mans, France, is the venue for the famous 24 Hours of Le Mans race.

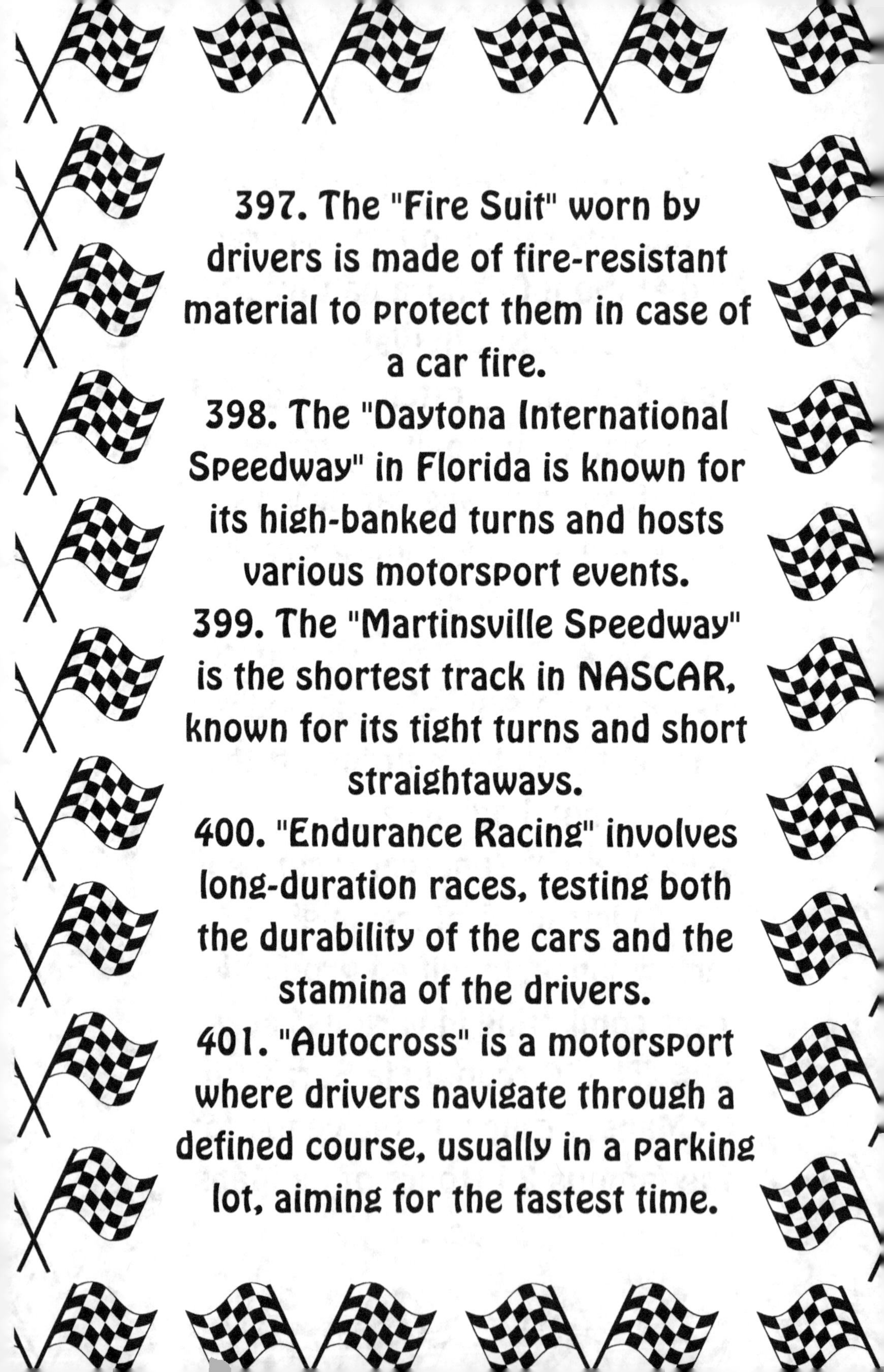

397. The "Fire Suit" worn by drivers is made of fire-resistant material to protect them in case of a car fire.

398. The "Daytona International Speedway" in Florida is known for its high-banked turns and hosts various motorsport events.

399. The "Martinsville Speedway" is the shortest track in NASCAR, known for its tight turns and short straightaways.

400. "Endurance Racing" involves long-duration races, testing both the durability of the cars and the stamina of the drivers.

401. "Autocross" is a motorsport where drivers navigate through a defined course, usually in a parking lot, aiming for the fastest time.

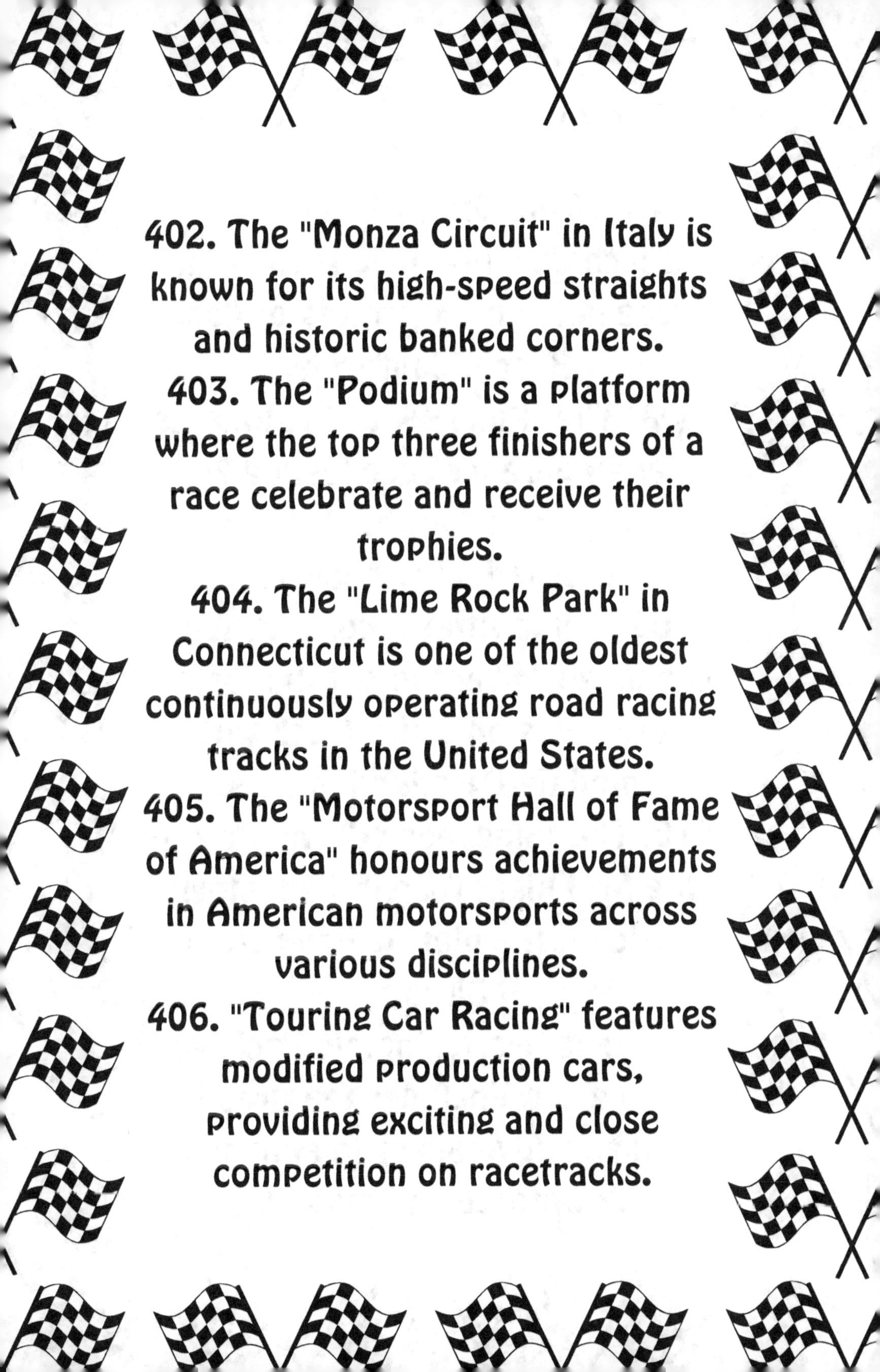

402. The "Monza Circuit" in Italy is known for its high-speed straights and historic banked corners.

403. The "Podium" is a platform where the top three finishers of a race celebrate and receive their trophies.

404. The "Lime Rock Park" in Connecticut is one of the oldest continuously operating road racing tracks in the United States.

405. The "Motorsport Hall of Fame of America" honours achievements in American motorsports across various disciplines.

406. "Touring Car Racing" features modified production cars, providing exciting and close competition on racetracks.

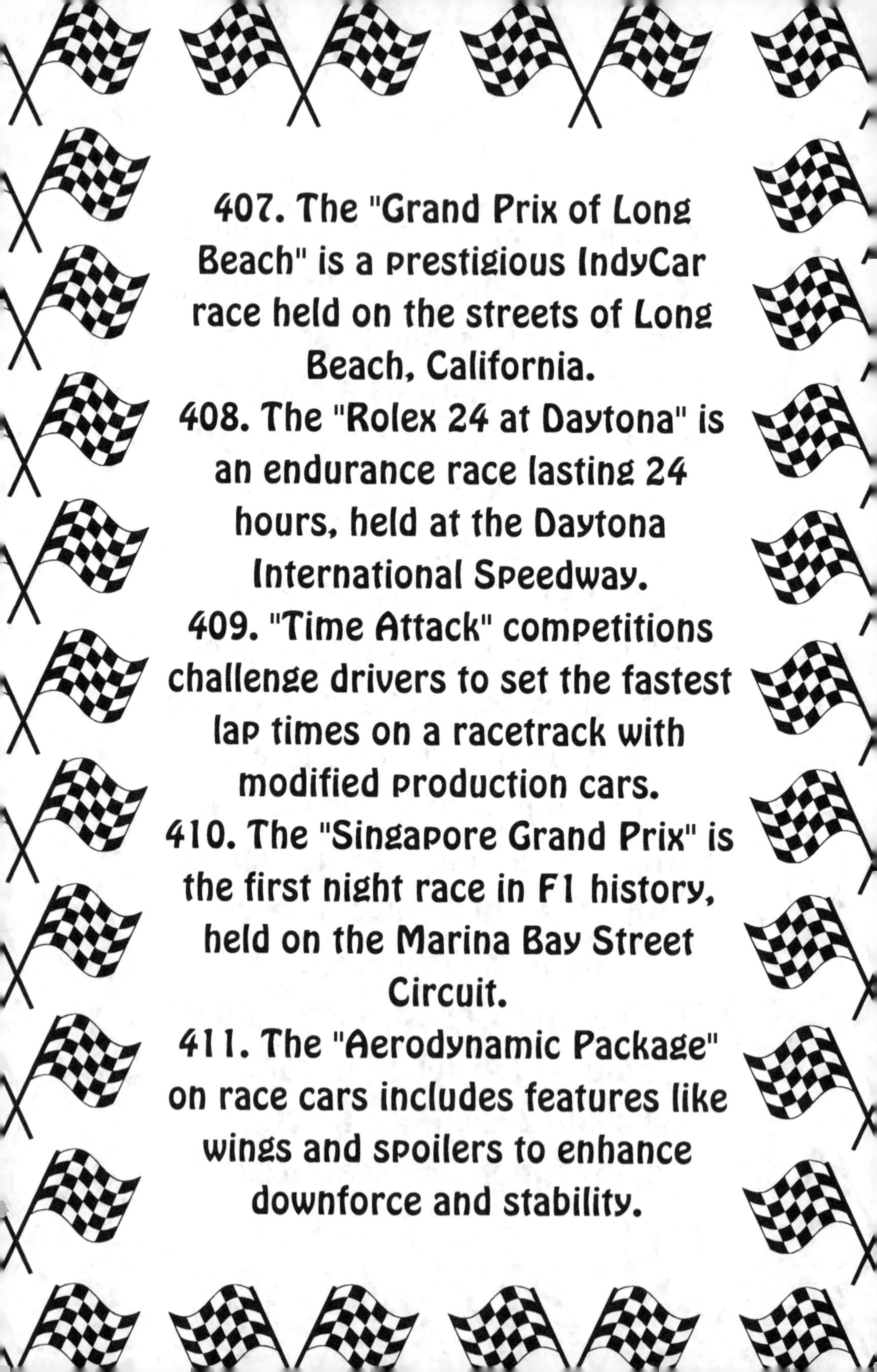

407. The "Grand Prix of Long Beach" is a prestigious IndyCar race held on the streets of Long Beach, California.

408. The "Rolex 24 at Daytona" is an endurance race lasting 24 hours, held at the Daytona International Speedway.

409. "Time Attack" competitions challenge drivers to set the fastest lap times on a racetrack with modified production cars.

410. The "Singapore Grand Prix" is the first night race in F1 history, held on the Marina Bay Street Circuit.

411. The "Aerodynamic Package" on race cars includes features like wings and spoilers to enhance downforce and stability.

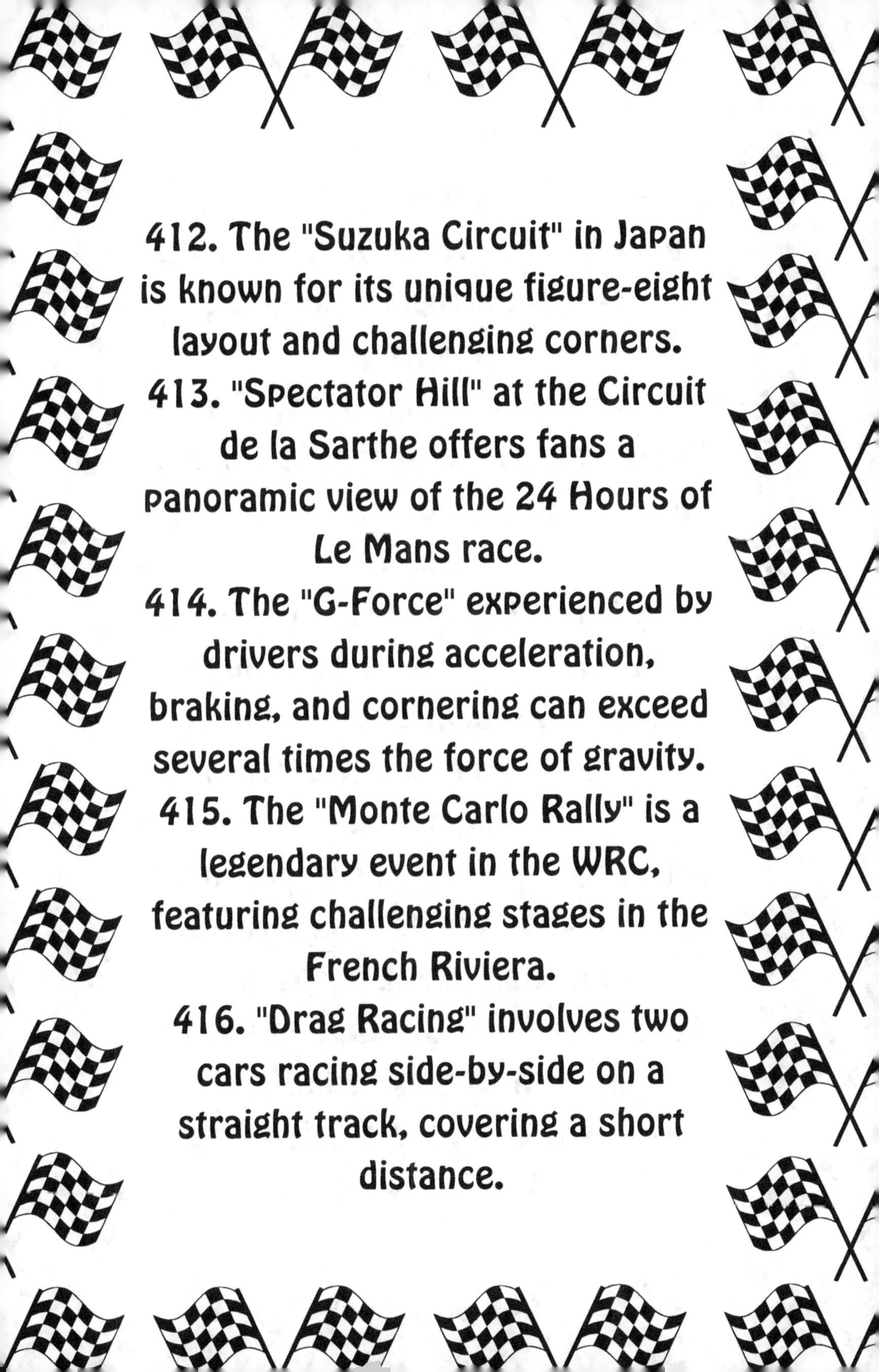

412. The "Suzuka Circuit" in Japan is known for its unique figure-eight layout and challenging corners.

413. "Spectator Hill" at the Circuit de la Sarthe offers fans a panoramic view of the 24 Hours of Le Mans race.

414. The "G-Force" experienced by drivers during acceleration, braking, and cornering can exceed several times the force of gravity.

415. The "Monte Carlo Rally" is a legendary event in the WRC, featuring challenging stages in the French Riviera.

416. "Drag Racing" involves two cars racing side-by-side on a straight track, covering a short distance.

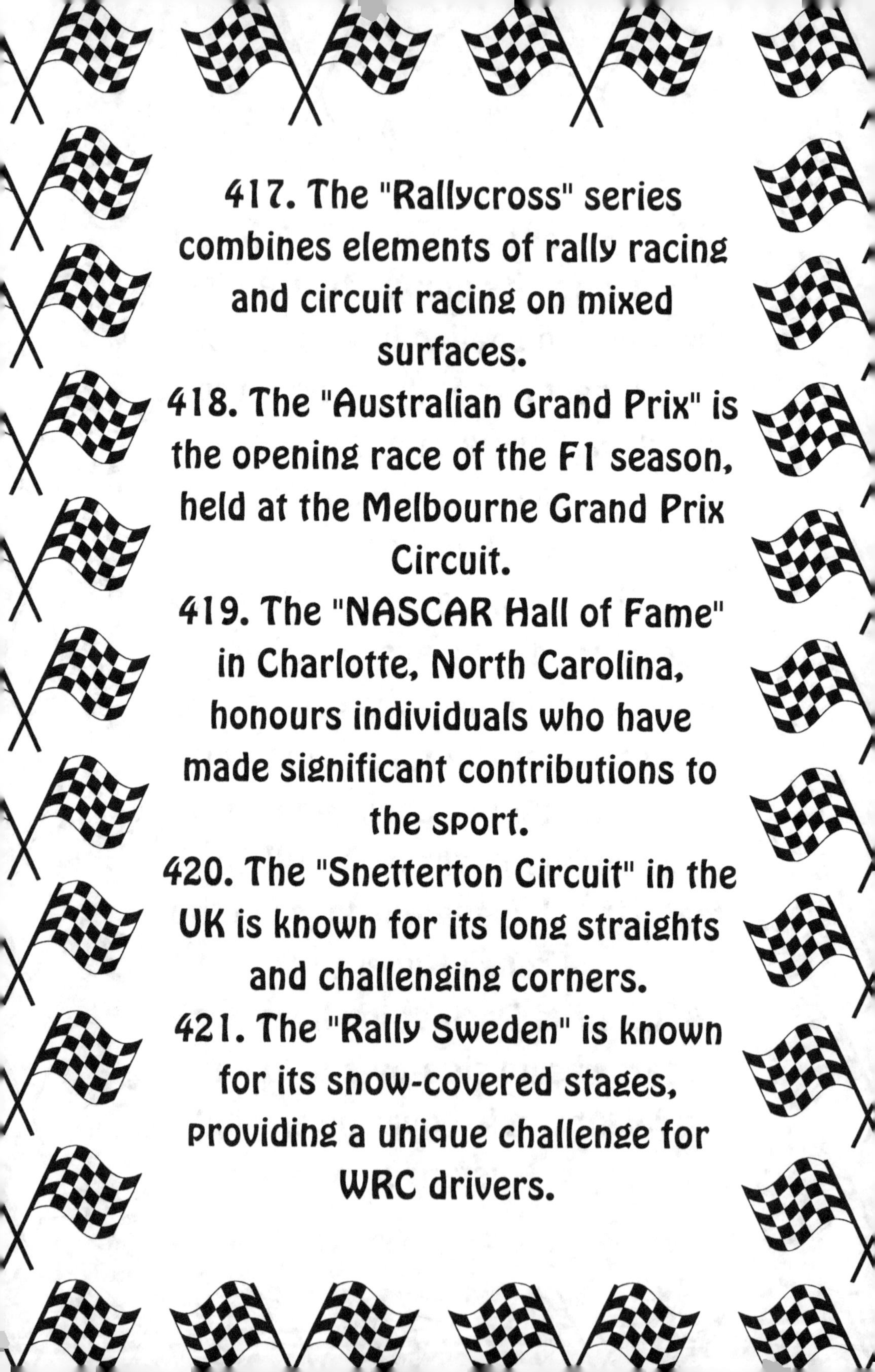

417. The "Rallycross" series combines elements of rally racing and circuit racing on mixed surfaces.

418. The "Australian Grand Prix" is the opening race of the F1 season, held at the Melbourne Grand Prix Circuit.

419. The "NASCAR Hall of Fame" in Charlotte, North Carolina, honours individuals who have made significant contributions to the sport.

420. The "Snetterton Circuit" in the UK is known for its long straights and challenging corners.

421. The "Rally Sweden" is known for its snow-covered stages, providing a unique challenge for WRC drivers.

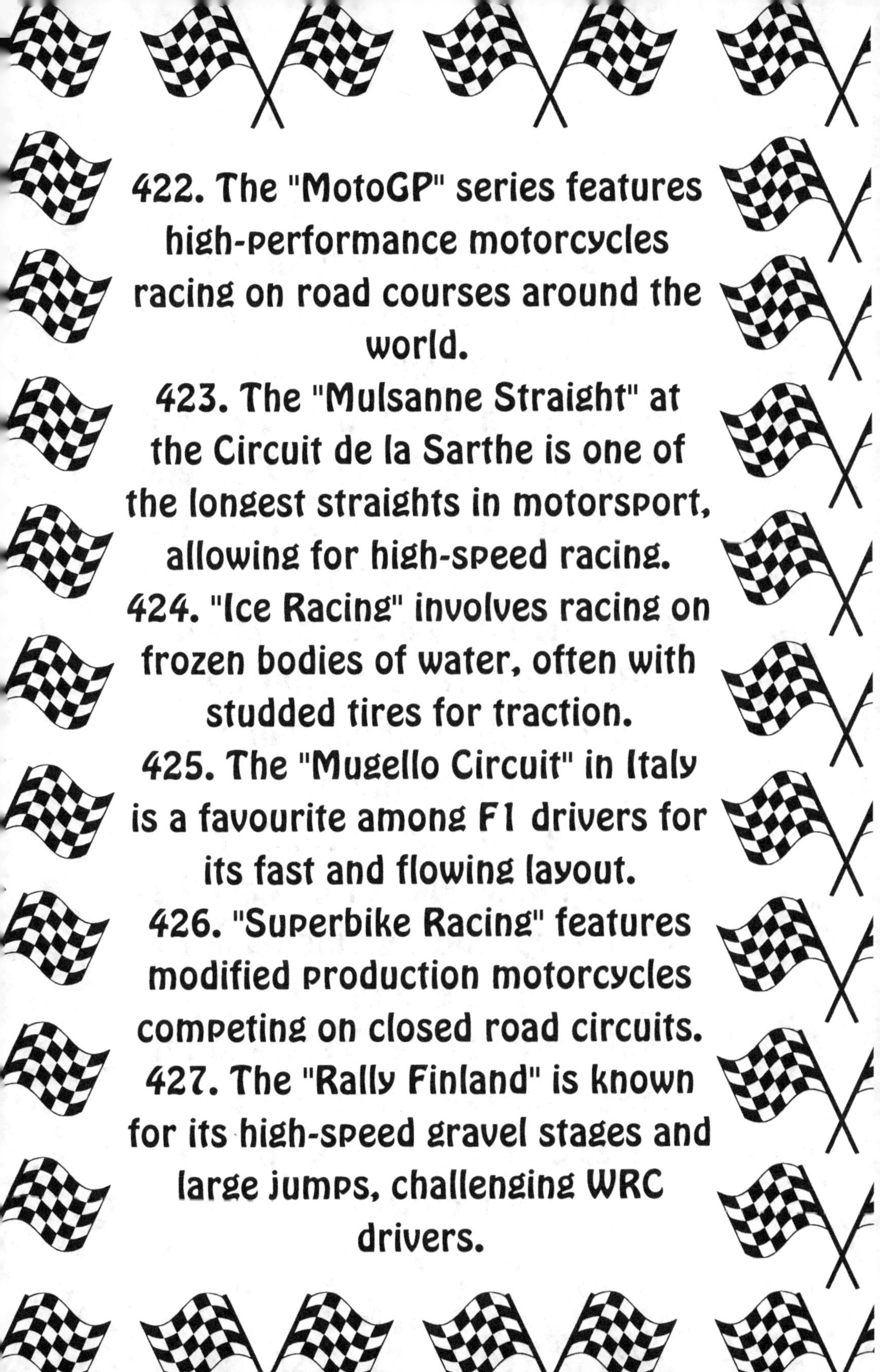

422. The "MotoGP" series features high-performance motorcycles racing on road courses around the world.

423. The "Mulsanne Straight" at the Circuit de la Sarthe is one of the longest straights in motorsport, allowing for high-speed racing.

424. "Ice Racing" involves racing on frozen bodies of water, often with studded tires for traction.

425. The "Mugello Circuit" in Italy is a favourite among F1 drivers for its fast and flowing layout.

426. "Superbike Racing" features modified production motorcycles competing on closed road circuits.

427. The "Rally Finland" is known for its high-speed gravel stages and large jumps, challenging WRC drivers.

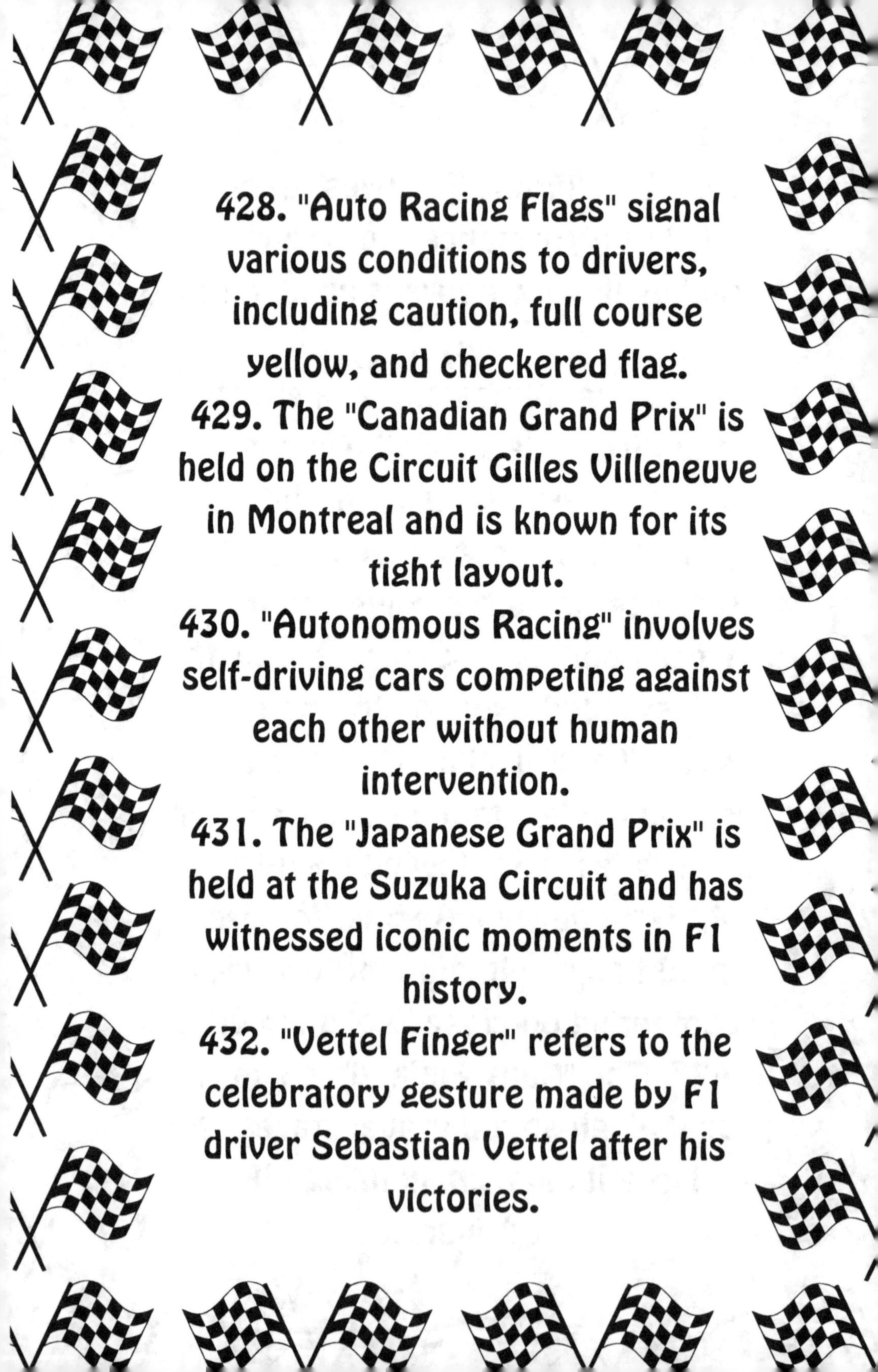

428. "Auto Racing Flags" signal various conditions to drivers, including caution, full course yellow, and checkered flag.

429. The "Canadian Grand Prix" is held on the Circuit Gilles Villeneuve in Montreal and is known for its tight layout.

430. "Autonomous Racing" involves self-driving cars competing against each other without human intervention.

431. The "Japanese Grand Prix" is held at the Suzuka Circuit and has witnessed iconic moments in F1 history.

432. "Vettel Finger" refers to the celebratory gesture made by F1 driver Sebastian Vettel after his victories.

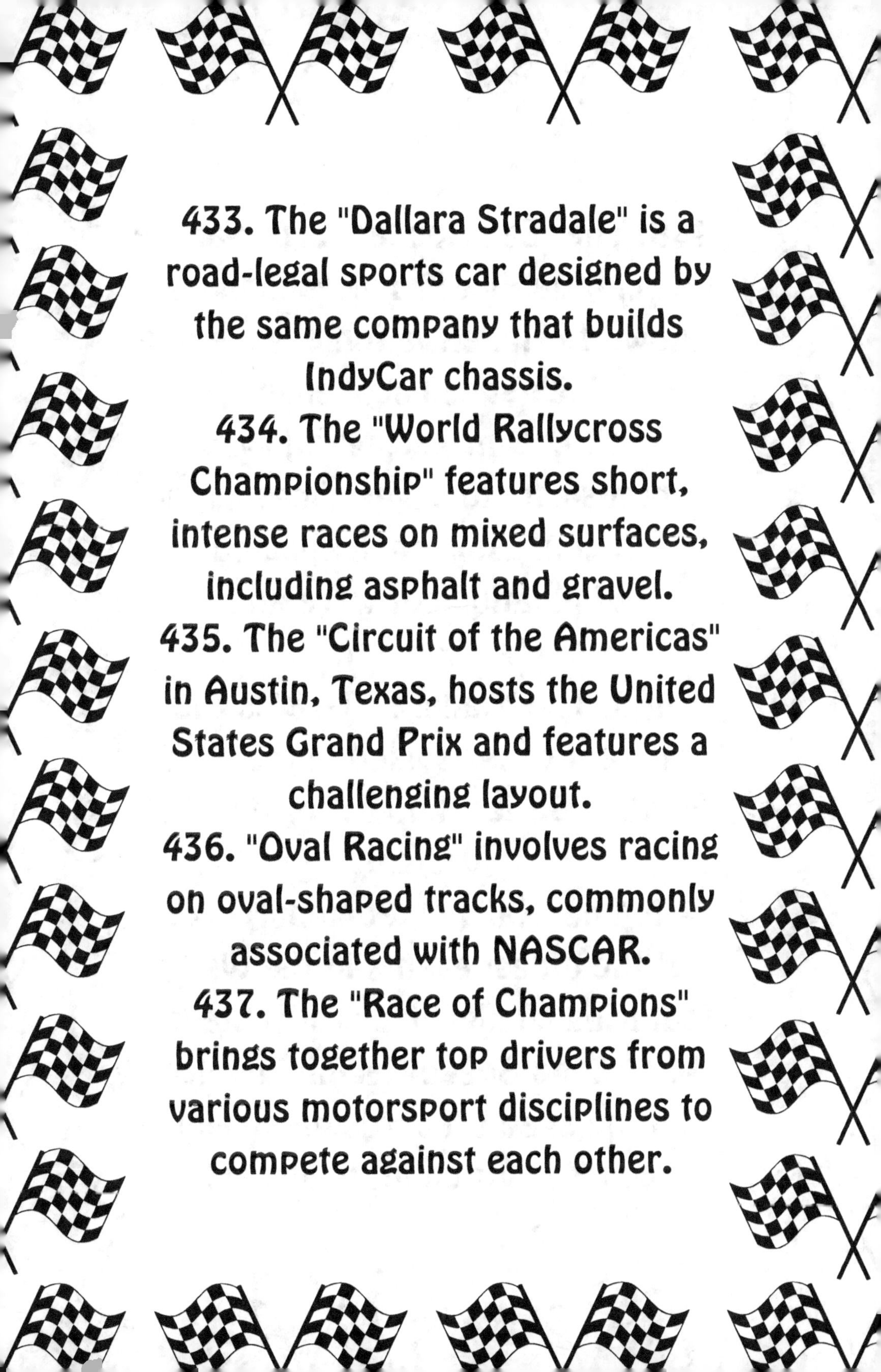

433. The "Dallara Stradale" is a road-legal sports car designed by the same company that builds IndyCar chassis.

434. The "World Rallycross Championship" features short, intense races on mixed surfaces, including asphalt and gravel.

435. The "Circuit of the Americas" in Austin, Texas, hosts the United States Grand Prix and features a challenging layout.

436. "Oval Racing" involves racing on oval-shaped tracks, commonly associated with NASCAR.

437. The "Race of Champions" brings together top drivers from various motorsport disciplines to compete against each other.

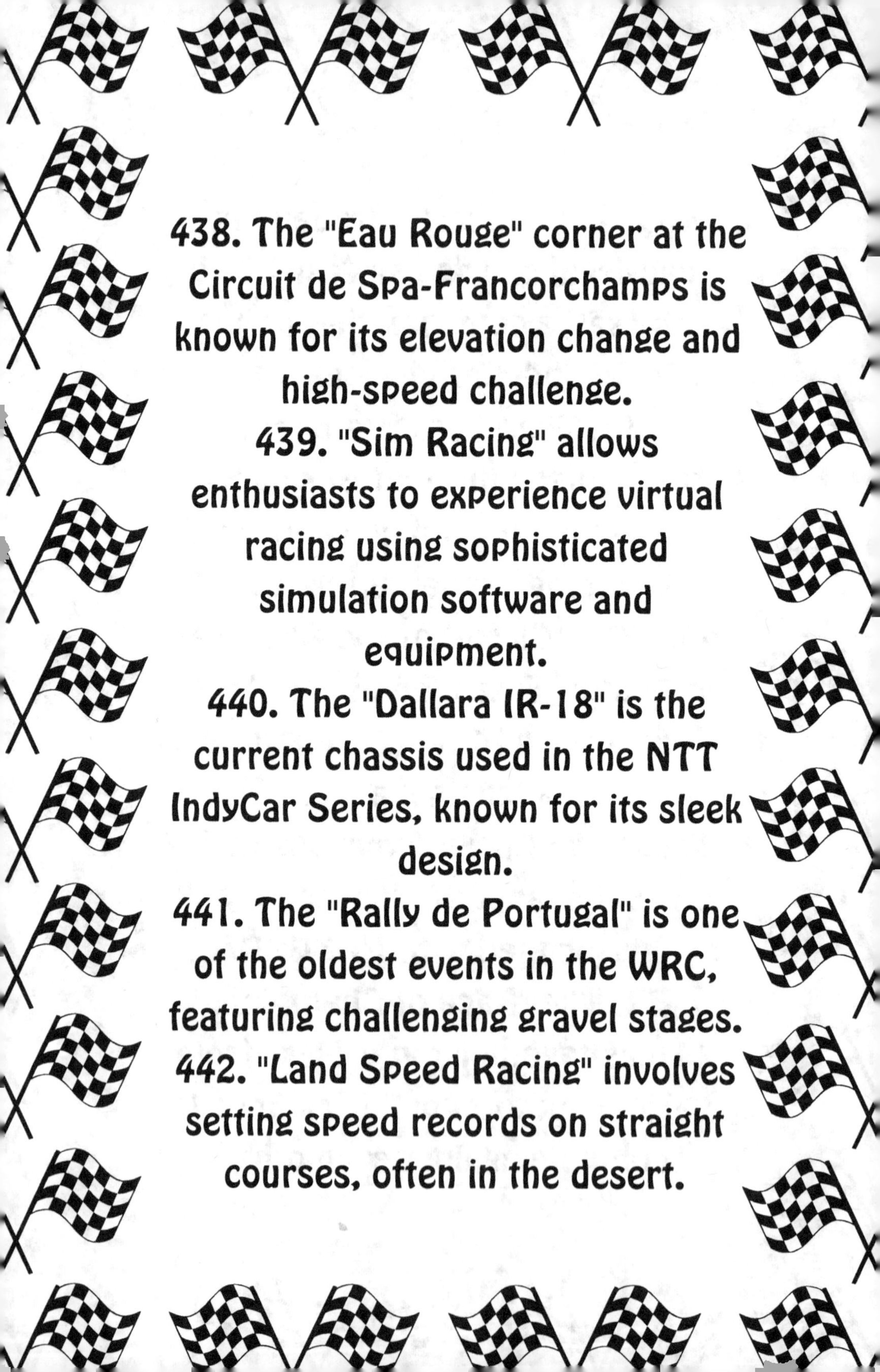

438. The "Eau Rouge" corner at the Circuit de Spa-Francorchamps is known for its elevation change and high-speed challenge.

439. "Sim Racing" allows enthusiasts to experience virtual racing using sophisticated simulation software and equipment.

440. The "Dallara IR-18" is the current chassis used in the NTT IndyCar Series, known for its sleek design.

441. The "Rally de Portugal" is one of the oldest events in the WRC, featuring challenging gravel stages.

442. "Land Speed Racing" involves setting speed records on straight courses, often in the desert.

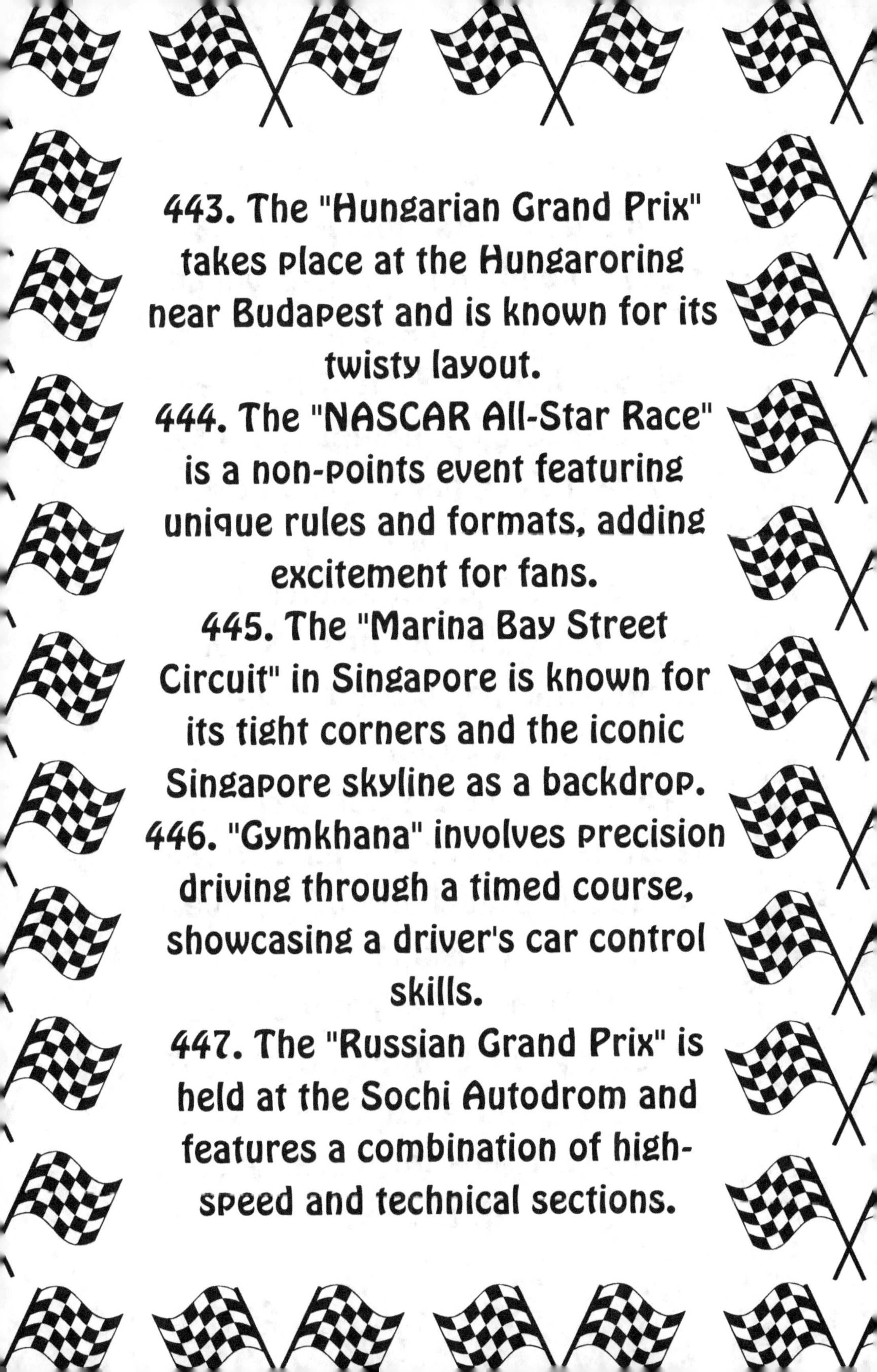

443. The "Hungarian Grand Prix" takes place at the Hungaroring near Budapest and is known for its twisty layout.

444. The "NASCAR All-Star Race" is a non-points event featuring unique rules and formats, adding excitement for fans.

445. The "Marina Bay Street Circuit" in Singapore is known for its tight corners and the iconic Singapore skyline as a backdrop.

446. "Gymkhana" involves precision driving through a timed course, showcasing a driver's car control skills.

447. The "Russian Grand Prix" is held at the Sochi Autodrom and features a combination of high-speed and technical sections.

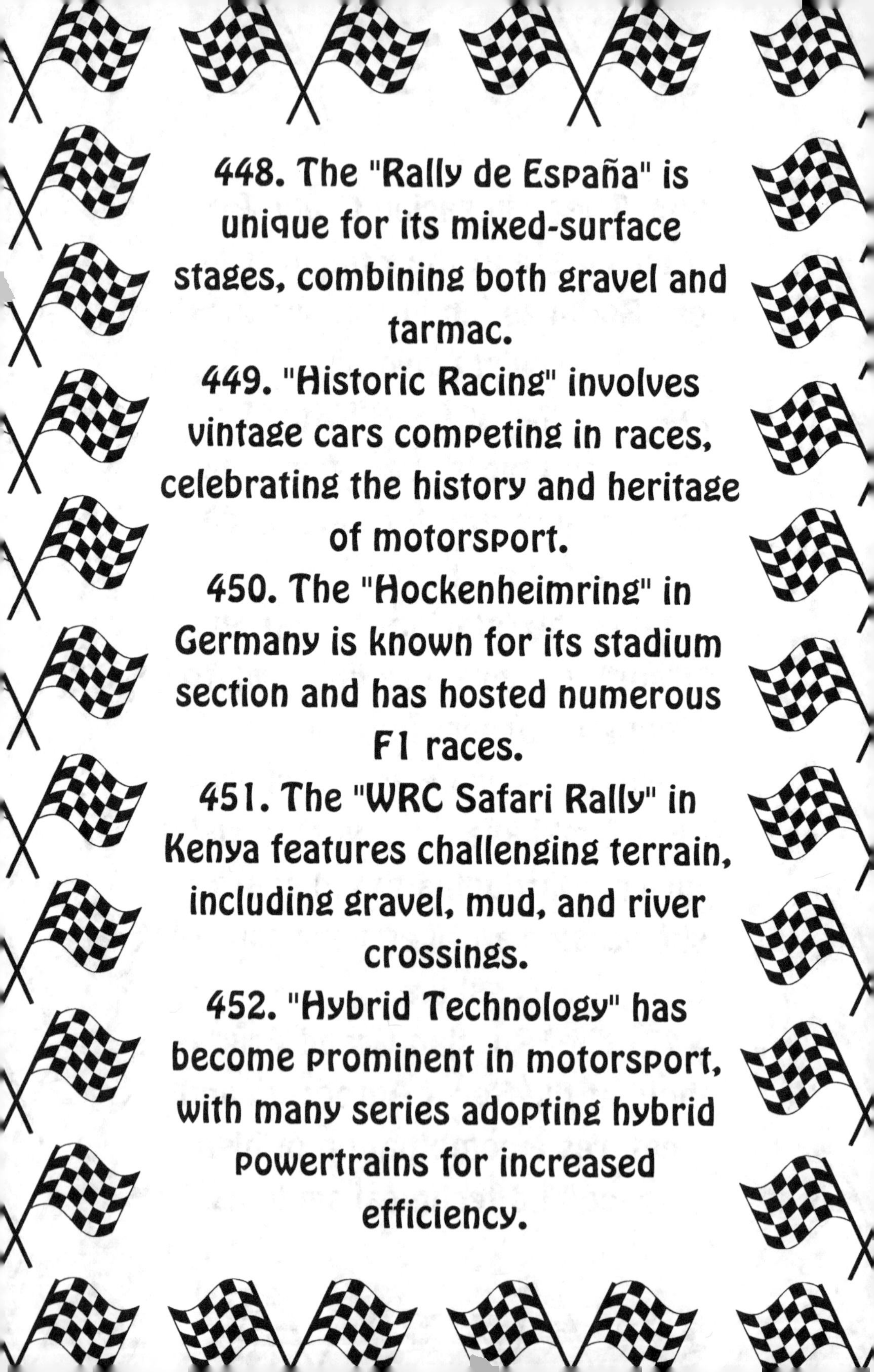

448. The "Rally de España" is unique for its mixed-surface stages, combining both gravel and tarmac.

449. "Historic Racing" involves vintage cars competing in races, celebrating the history and heritage of motorsport.

450. The "Hockenheimring" in Germany is known for its stadium section and has hosted numerous F1 races.

451. The "WRC Safari Rally" in Kenya features challenging terrain, including gravel, mud, and river crossings.

452. "Hybrid Technology" has become prominent in motorsport, with many series adopting hybrid powertrains for increased efficiency.

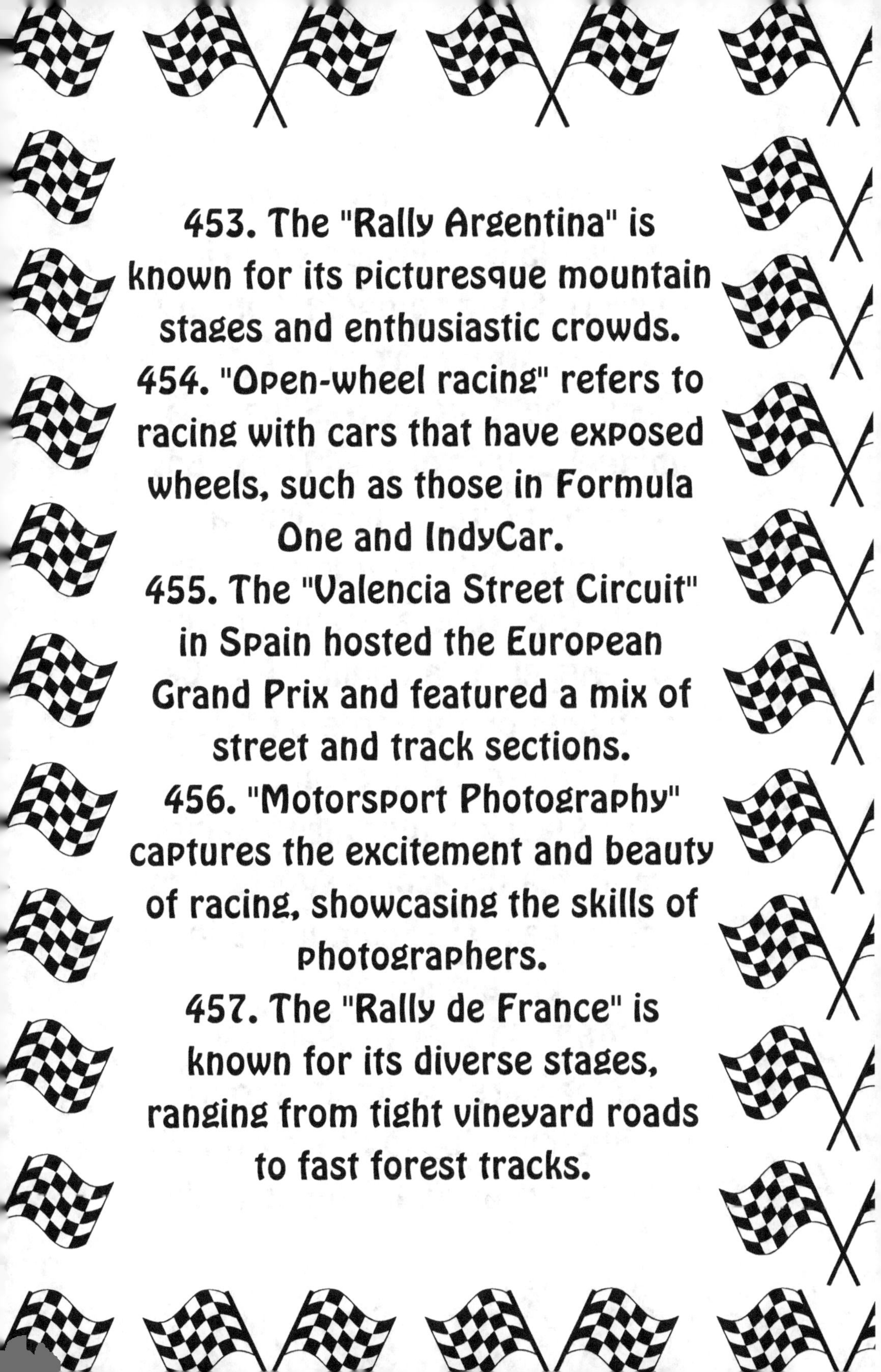

453. The "Rally Argentina" is known for its picturesque mountain stages and enthusiastic crowds.
454. "Open-wheel racing" refers to racing with cars that have exposed wheels, such as those in Formula One and IndyCar.
455. The "Valencia Street Circuit" in Spain hosted the European Grand Prix and featured a mix of street and track sections.
456. "Motorsport Photography" captures the excitement and beauty of racing, showcasing the skills of photographers.
457. The "Rally de France" is known for its diverse stages, ranging from tight vineyard roads to fast forest tracks.

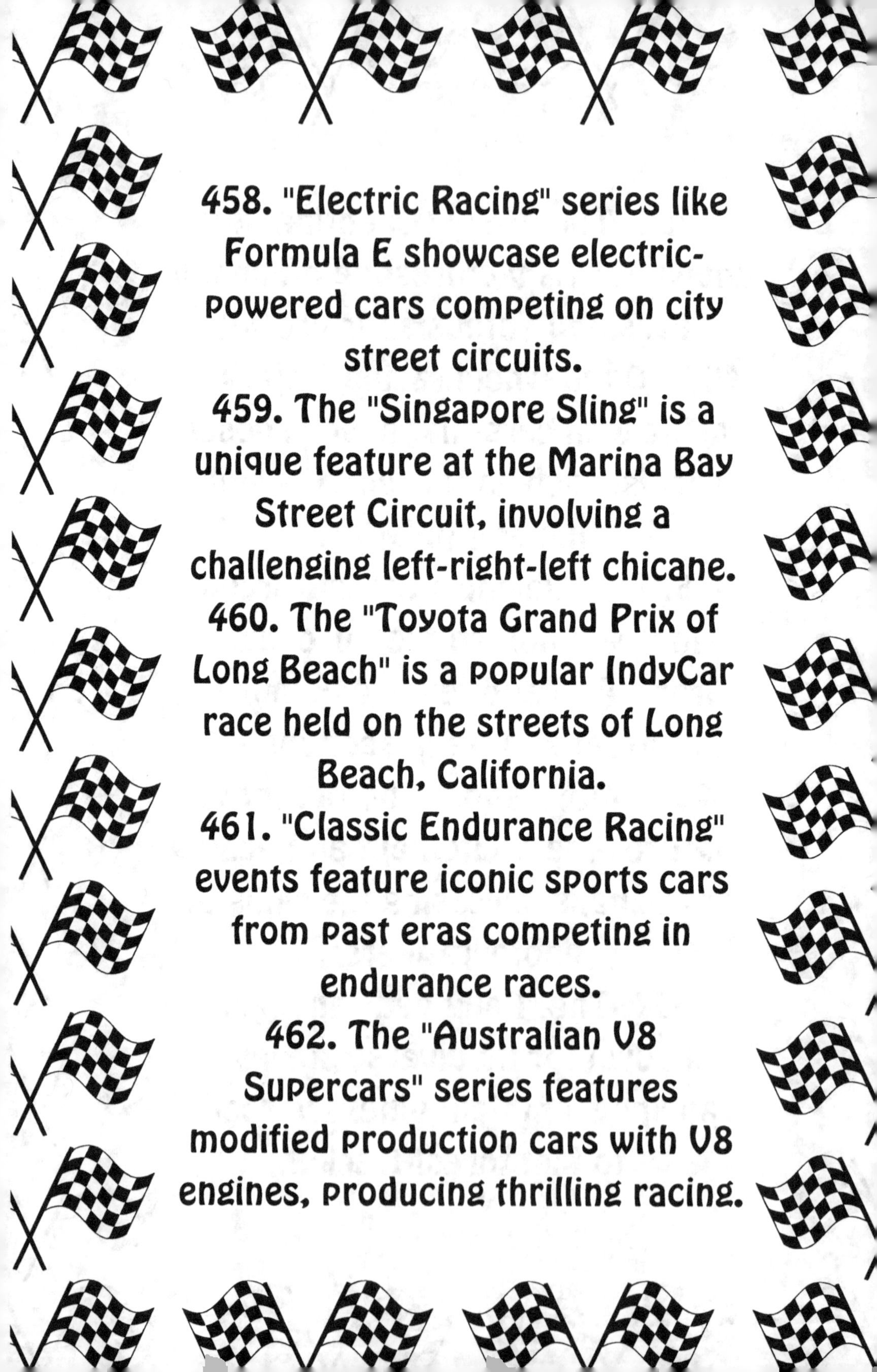

458. "Electric Racing" series like Formula E showcase electric-powered cars competing on city street circuits.

459. The "Singapore Sling" is a unique feature at the Marina Bay Street Circuit, involving a challenging left-right-left chicane.

460. The "Toyota Grand Prix of Long Beach" is a popular IndyCar race held on the streets of Long Beach, California.

461. "Classic Endurance Racing" events feature iconic sports cars from past eras competing in endurance races.

462. The "Australian V8 Supercars" series features modified production cars with V8 engines, producing thrilling racing.

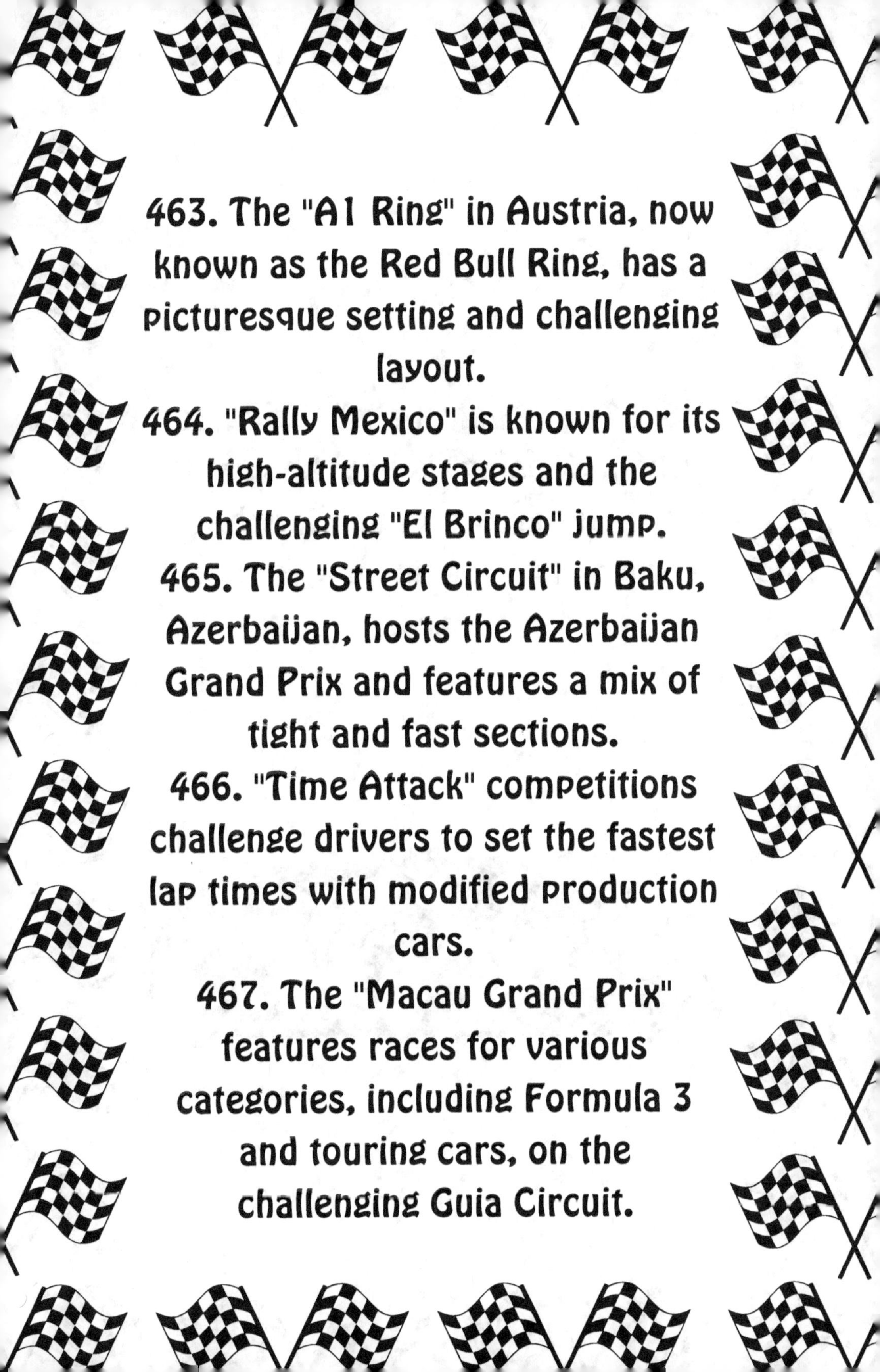

463. The "A1 Ring" in Austria, now known as the Red Bull Ring, has a picturesque setting and challenging layout.

464. "Rally Mexico" is known for its high-altitude stages and the challenging "El Brinco" jump.

465. The "Street Circuit" in Baku, Azerbaijan, hosts the Azerbaijan Grand Prix and features a mix of tight and fast sections.

466. "Time Attack" competitions challenge drivers to set the fastest lap times with modified production cars.

467. The "Macau Grand Prix" features races for various categories, including Formula 3 and touring cars, on the challenging Guia Circuit.

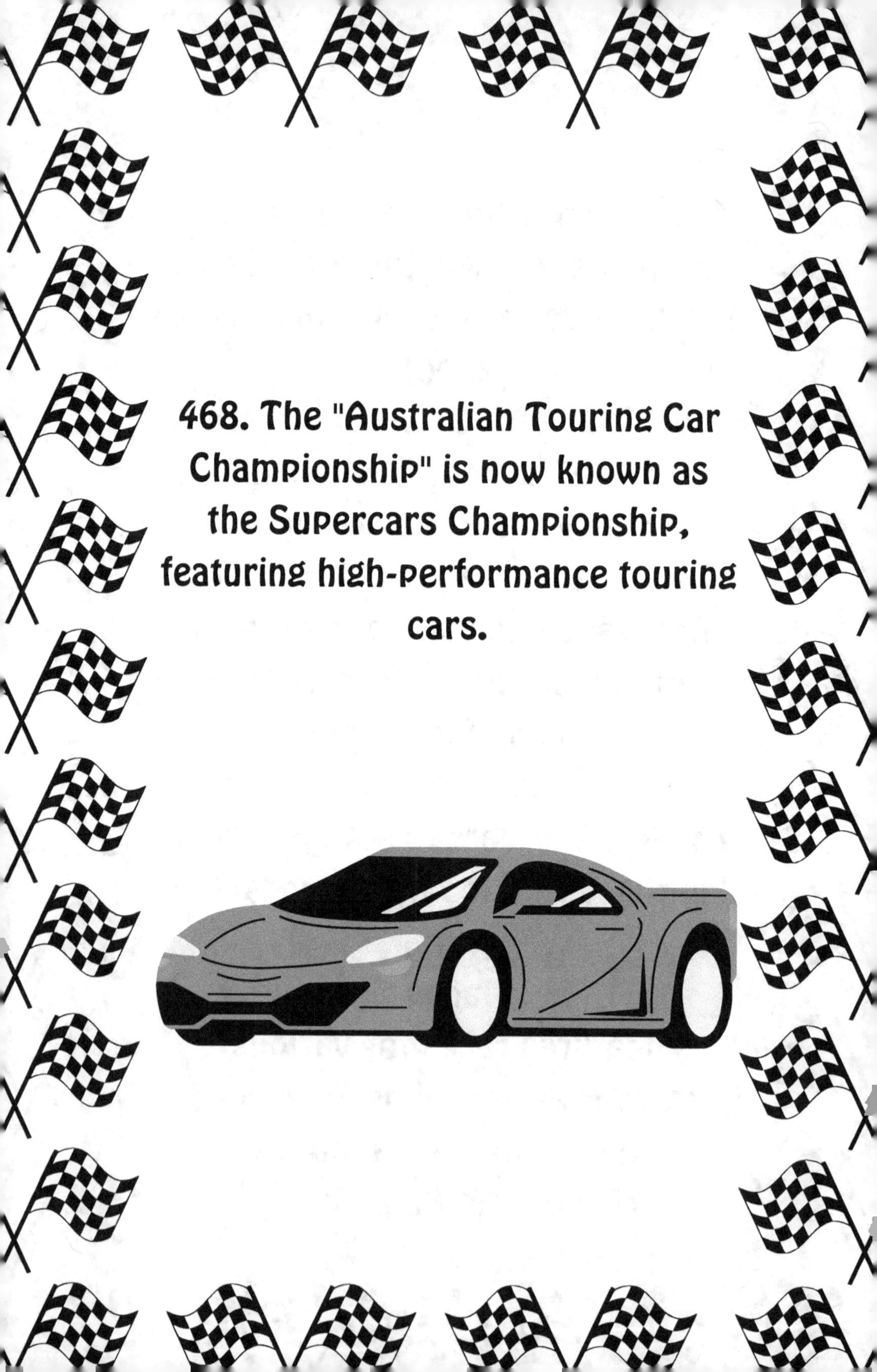

468. The "Australian Touring Car Championship" is now known as the Supercars Championship, featuring high-performance touring cars.

9 7 9 8 8 7 8 7 6 3 0 0 4